SWU-NAP- 014

UNIFORMS OF RUSSIAN ARMY DURING THE NAPOLEONIC WAR VOL.9

UNDER THE REIGN OF ALEXANDER I
EMPEROR OF RUSSIA BETWEEN 1801 AND 1825
ARMY INFANTRY: MUSKETEERS, JAGER& MARINE REGIMENTS

From the Viskovatov's greatest work:
"Historical description of the clothing and arms of the Russian Army"

English translation by Mark Conrad

SOLDIERSHOP PUBLISHING

AUTHOR

Aleksandr Vasilevich Viskovatov born 22 April (4 May New Style) 1804, died 27 February (11 March) 1858 in St. Petersburg, Russian military historian. He graduated from the 1st Cadet Corps and served in the artillery, the hydrographic depot of the Naval Ministry, and then in the Department of Military Educational Institutions. He mainly studied historical artifacts and the histories of military units. Viskovatov's greatest work was the Historical Description of the Clothing and Arms of the Russian Army.

TRANSLATOR

Mark Conrad is an American historian with a great interest for all the Russian history.

Title: **UNIFORMS OF RUSSIAN ARMY DURING THE NAPOLEONIC WAR VOL. 9 -**
Army Infantry: Musketeers, jagers & marine regiments 1801-1825
By A.V.Viskovatov. English translation by Mark Conrad. First edition by Soldiershop.
Cover & Art Design: Luca S. Cristini. Plates re-colorations by Anna Cristini
ISBN code: 978-88-932709922

Published by Soldiershop publishing, via Padre Davide, 7 - 24050 Zanica (BG) ITALY. www.soldiershop.com

UNIFORMS
OF THE RUSSIAN
ARMY DURING THE
NAPOLEONIC WAR VOL.9

UNDER THE REIGN OF ALEXANDER I EMPEROR OF RUSSIA BETWEEN 1801 AND 1825

*

Army infantry: Musketeers, jager & marine regiments

Alexander I (1802 c.) By F.Kruger (1837, Hermitage)

HISTORICAL DESCRIPTION OF THE CLOTHING AND ARMS
OF THE RUSSIAN ARMY - A.V. VISKOVATOV
(First English translation by Mark Conrad)

Soldiershop is glad to presents the complete collection of the great job made by A.V. Viskovatov dedicated to the uniforms and weapons belonging to the Russian army during the Napoleonic period, until 1825. The time we considered corresponds to the reigns of two Tzars: Paul I, who reigned since 1769 until his murder on the 23rd of March 1801, and his son Aleksandr Pavlovi□ Romanov, that with the title of Alexander I, sat on the throne until the 1st December 1825.

Our reprint in based on the original 19th century volumes, to be precise the volumes from 7 to 9 are dedicated to the reign of Paul I; this first part is distributed on 7 volumes, having a numbering from 1 to 7. From number 10 to 18 of the original volumes, the second part is dedicated to the Russian troops under Alexander I. These still being worked on and they will be soon ready, distributed on twenty volumes approximately. Our new edition, the first ever published in English, both on paper and digital format, boasts a large number of color plates, many of them unpublished and coloured by our team of expert artists and scholars of uniformology. Each volume is based on 50/70 plates, always accompanied by the original translated text which describes the uniforms, the organization and the armament of the Russian army of the period.

A unique work in its genre, a must have in any respecting collection!
Aleksandr Vasilevich Viskovatov born 22 April (4 May New Style) 1804, died 27 February (11 March) 1858 in St. Petersburg, Russian military historian. He graduated from the 1st Cadet Corps and served in the artillery, the hydrographic depot of the Naval Ministry, and then in the Department of Military Educational Institutions.

He mainly studied historical artifacts and the histories of military units. Viskovatov's greatest work was the Historical Description of the Clothing and Arms of the Russian Army (Vols. 1-30, St. Petersburg, 1841-62; 2nd ed. Vols. 1-34, St. Petersburg - Novosibirsk - Leningrad, 1899-1948). This work is based on a great quantity of archival documents and contains four thousand colored illustrations.

Viskovatov was the author of Chronicles of the Russian Army (Books 1-20, St. Petersburg, 1834-42) and Chronicles of the Russian Imperial Army (Parts 1-7, St. Petersburg, 1852). He collected valuable material on the history of the Russian navy which went into A Short Overview of Russian Naval Campaigns and General Voyages to the End of the XVII Century (St. Petersburg, 1864; 2nd edition Moscow, 1946). Together with A.I. Mikhailovskii-Danilevskii he helped prepare and create the Military Gallery in the Winter Palace.

He wrote the historical military inscriptions for the walls of the Hall of St. George in the Great Palace of the Kremlin. (From the article in the Soviet Military Encyclopedia.)

CONTENTS

*

Preface pag. 5

*

Russian Army: Organization 1801-1825 2nd part pag. 7

The Army Infantry pag. 7
Notes 1st part pag. 22
Musketeers regiments 1801-1825 pag. 25
Marine & Jager regiments 1801-1825 pag. 35
Grenadier Jager, or Carabinier, regiments 1801-1825 pa. 40
Notes to illustrations pag. 40
Notes 2nd part pag. 42

*

PLATES pag. 45

RUSSIAN ARMY,
Organization 1801-1825 1st part

CHANGES IN THE COMPOSITION AND NOMENCLATURE OF ALL FORCES, FROM 1801 TO 1825

Military Land Forces on 12 March, 1801 - I.   Army Infantry.

I. ARMY INFANTRY (FIRST PART ON VOLUME 8)

11 March 1813– The Borodinskii [Borodino] and Tarutinskii [Tarutino]Pekhotnye polki were established, assigned to the 23rd Division (56).

16 March 1813– The 1-i, 2-i, 3-i, and 4-i Morskie polki [Marine regiments], each consisting of three four-company battalions, and the four-company Kaspiiskii Morskoi batalion [Caspian Marine Battalion] were transferred from the Navy Department [Morskoe vedomstvo] to the Military-Land [i.e. Army] Department [Voenno-Sukhoputnoe vedomstvo]. In 1812 the first three of these were already in the 25th Infantry Division (57).

13 April 1813– For their distinction during the 1812 campaign, the Life-Grenadier and Pavlovsk Grenadier Regiments became part of the Guards, and the Kexholm and Pernau Infantry, for similar distinction, became Grenadiers (58).

11 July 1813– New regiments were established: the Krasinskii, Rostovskii, Izmailskii and Benderskii [Bendery] Pekhotnye polki [Infantry regiments] and the 51-i, 52-i, and 53-i Yegerskie polki [Jäger regiments], of which the Krasinskii and the 51st joined the 23rd Infantry Division, and from the remaining five along with the 4th Marine Regiment was formed a new division titled the 28th Infantry. The 12 Zapasnyi and 8 Reservnyi battalions of the 8th, 10th, 12th, and 22nd Divisions, left in Bessarabia and the New Russia Territory, were used to form these regiments (59).

4 November 1813– Of the regiments listed above, the Krasinskii was named the 54-i Yegerskii [54th Jägers], the Rostovskii – the 55-i, and the Benderskii – the 56-i (60).

3 April 1814– The 1st, 3rd, 8th, 14th, 26th, and 29th Jäger regiments, in recognition of the distinction they showed in the past war with France, were titled Grenadier Jägers [Grenaderskie Yegerskie], with retention of their previous numbers and with inclusion into the Grenadier Corps [Grenaderskii Korpus], which at this time was formed from the three Grenadier divisions, with regiments assigned to these divisions as follows:

In the 1st Grenadier Division — Yekaterinoslavl, Graf Arakcheev's, Kexholm, and Pernau Gren., and 1st and 3rd Grenadier Jägers.
In the 2nd Grenadier Division Kiev, Moscow, St.-Petersburg, and Taurica Grenadiers, and 8th and 14th Grenadier Jägers.
In the 3rd Grenadier DivisionAstrakhan, Phanagoria, Siberia, and Little Russia Grenadiers, and 26th and 29th Grenadier Jägers.

To replace the six Jäger regiments removed to these divisions, regiments were reassigned as follows: from the 23rd Division to the 6th Division – the 54th Jägers; from the 28th to the 15th – the 52nd Jägers; from the 28th, again, to the 10th – the 53rd Jägers; from the 28th, again, to the 14th – the 55th Jägers; from the 28th, again, to the 22nd – the 56th Jägers; and from the 28th, again, to the 11th – the 57th Jägers. The remaining regiment of the 28th Division, the 4th Marines, transferred to the 23rd Division in place of the reassigned 54th Jägers, and then the number of the disbanded 28th Infantry Division was adopted by the former 3rd Infantry Division (61).

29 August 1814 – With the confirmation of a new distribution of corps, divisions, and brigades to the armies, Army infantry regiments were assigned to these as follows:

Grenadier Corps:
1st Grenadier Div., in the 1st Brigade — Yekaterinoslavl and Graf Arakcheev's Grenadiers.
  — — 2nd — — — Kexholm and Pernau Grenadiers.
  — — 3rd — — — 1st and 3rd Grenadier Jägers.
2nd Grenadier Div., in the 1st Brigade — Kiev and Moscow Grenadiers.
  — — 2nd — — — St.-Petersburg and Taurica Grenadiers.
  — — 3rd — — — 8th and 14th Grenadier Jägers.
3rd Grenadier Div., in the 1st Brigade — Astrakhan and Phanagoria Grenadiers.
  — — 2nd — — — Siberia and Little Russia Grenadiers.
  — — 3rd — — — 26th and 29th Grenadier Jägers.

1st Infantry Corps:

5th Infantry Div., in the 1st Brigade — Pernau and Mogilev Infantry.
— — 2nd — — — Sevsk and Kaluga Infantry.
— — 3rd — — — 23rd and 24th Jägers.
14th Infantry Div., in the 1st Brigade — Tula and Navaginsk Infantry.
— — 2nd — — — Tenginsk and Estonia Infantry.
— — 3rd — — — 25th and 55th Jägers.
6th Infantry Div., in the 1st Brigade — Bryansk and Nizovsk Infantry.
— — 2nd — — — Azov and Kopore Infantry.
— — 3rd — — — 18th and 54th Jägers.

2nd Infantry Corps:

4th Infantry Div., in the 1st Brigade — Tobolsk and Minsk Infantry.
— — 2nd — — — Volhynia and Kremenchug Infantry.
— — 3rd — — — 4th and 34th Jägers.
28th Infantry Div., in the 1st Brigade — Chernigov and Murom Infantry.
— — 2nd — — — Reval and Selenginsk Infantry.
— — 3rd — — — 20th and 21st Jägers.
25th Infantry Div., in the 1st Brigade — 1st and 2nd Marines.
— — 2nd — — — 3rd Marines and Voronezh Infantry.
— — 3rd — — — 31st and 47th Jägers.

3rd Infantry Corps:

27th Infantry Div., in the 1st Brigade — Odessa and Tarnopol Infantry.
— — 2nd — — — Vilna and Simbirsk Infantry.
— — 3rd — — — 49th and 50th Jägers.
7th Infantry Div., in the 1st Brigade — Pskov and Moscow Infantry.
— — 2nd — — — Sofiya and Libau Infantry.
— — 3rd — — — 11th and 56th Jägers.
24th Infantry Div., in the 1st Brigade — Shirvan and Ufa Infantry.
— — 2nd — — — Tomsk and Butyrskii Infantry.
— — 3rd — — — 19th and 40th Jägers.

4th Infantry Corps:

11th Infantry Div., in the 1st Brigade — Yelets and Polotsk Infantry.
— — 2nd — — — Rylsk and Yekaterinburg Infantry.
— — 3rd — — — 33rd and 57th Jägers.
17th Infantry Div., in the 1st Brigade — Ryazan and Brest Infantry.
— — 2nd — — — Villmanstrand and Belozersk Infantry.
— — 3rd — — — 30th and 48th Jägers.
23rd Infantry Div., in the 1st Brigade — Uglich Infantry and 35th Jägers.
— — 2nd — — — Borodino and Tarutino Infantry.
— — 3rd — — — Penza Infantry and 51st Jägers.

5th Infantry Corps:

12th Infantry Div., in the 1st Brigade — Smolensk and Narva Infantry.
— — 2nd — — — Aleksopol and New Ingermanland Infantry.
— — 3rd — — — 6th and 41st Jägers.
26th Infantry Div., in the 1st Brigade — Nizhnii-Novgorod and Ladoga Infantry.
— — 2nd — — — Poltava and Orel Infantry.
— — 3rd — — — 5th and 42nd Jägers.
15th Infantry Div., in the 1st Brigade — Vitebsk and Kozlov Infantry.
— — 2nd — — — Kolyvan and Kura Infantry.
— — 3rd — — — 13th and 52nd Jägers.

6th Infantry Corps:

8th Infantry Div., in the 1st Brigade — Archangel and Schlüsselburg Infantry.
— — 2nd — — — Old Ingermanland and Ukraine Infantry.
— — 3rd — — — 7th and 37th Jägers.

10th Infantry Div., in the 1st Brigade — Crimea and Bialystok Infantry.
  — — 2nd — — — Yaroslavl and Kursk Infantry.
  — — 3rd — — — 39th and 53rd Jägers.
9th Infantry Div., in the 1st Brigade — Nasheburg and Apsheron Infantry.
  — — 2nd — — — Ryazhsk and Yakutsk Infantry.
  — — 3rd — — — 10th and 38th Jägers.

7th Infantry Corps:
18th Infantry Div., in the 1st Brigade — Tambov and Vladimir Infantry.
  — — 2nd — — — Dnieper and Kostroma Infantry.
  — — 3rd — — — 28th and 32nd Jägers.
22nd Infantry Div., in the 1st Brigade — Vyatka and Staryi-Oskol Infantry.
  — — 2nd — — — Olonets and Viborg Infantry.
  — — 3rd — — — 45th and 56th Jägers.

8th Infantry Corps:
13th Infantry Div., in the 1st Brigade — Galich and Velikie-Luki Infantry.
  — — 2nd — — — Saratov Infantry and 4th Marines.
  — — 3rd — — — 12th and 22nd Jägers.
16th Infantry Div., in the 1st Brigade — Okhotsk and Nyslott Infantry.
  — — 2nd — — — Kamchatka and Mingrelia Infantry.
  — — 3rd — — — 27th and 43rd Jägers (62).

7 October 1814– The Kexholm Grenadier Regiment was titled the Grenaderskii Ego Velichestva Imperatora Avstriiskago polk [His Majesty the Emperor of Austria's Grenadier Regiment], and the St.-Petersburg Grenadiers—the Grenaderskii Ego Velichestva Korolya Prusskago polk [His Majesty the King of Prussia's Grenadier Regiment]. With this renaming of regiments in the Grenadier Corps, there was a new organization as follows:

1st Grenadier Division, 1st Brigade His Majesty the Emperor of Austria's and His Majesty the King of Prussia's Grenadiers.
  2nd — — — Graf Arakcheev's and Pernau Grenadiers.
  3rd — — — 1st and 3rd Grenadier Jägers.
2nd Grenadier Division, 1st Brigade Kiev and Taurica Grenadiers.
  2nd — — — Yekaterinoslavl and Moscow Grenadiers.
  3rd — — — 8th and 14th Grenadier Jägers.
3rd Grenadier Division, 1st Brigade Siberia and Little Russia Grenadiers.
  2nd — — — Phanagoria and Astrakhan Grenadiers.
  3rd — — — 26th and 29th Grenadier Jägers (63).

28 October 1814– With the division of the forces into two Armies, the 1st and the 2nd, they were assigned the following divisions of Army infantry:
  a.) In the 1st Army:
Grenadier Corps—2nd and 3rd Grenadier Divisions.
1st Infantry — — —5th, 6th, and 14th Infantry Divisions.
2nd Infantry — — 4th, 25th, and 28th — — — —
3rd Infantry — — —7th, 24th, and 27th — — — —
4th Infantry — — —11th, 17th, and 23rd — — — —
5th Infantry — — —15th and 26th — — — —
6th Infantry — — —8th and 10th — — — —
  b.) In the 2nd Army:
7th Infantry Corps—18th and 22nd Infantry Divisions.
8th Infantry — — — 13th and 16th — — — —

Of the other divisions, the 1st Grenadier was assigned to the Guards Corps; the 9th and 12th formed a special Corps in France; the 19th and 20th were, as before, with the Georgia Corps; and the 21st was stationed in Finland (64).

30 August 1815– Grenadier Jäger regiments were named Carabinier [Karabinernyi]: the 1st Grenadier Jägers – as the 1st Carabiniers, the 3rd – as the 2nd, the 8th – as the 3rd, the 14th – as the 4th, the 26th – as the 25th [sic, should be 5th – M.C.]; and the 29th – as the 6th (65).

5 October 1815– The Tarnopolskii Pekhotnyi polk [Tarnopol Infantry Regiment] was named the Zhitomirskii Pekhotnyi polk (66).

21 December 1815– The Georgia Corps was named the Separate Georgia Corps [Otdelnyi Gruzinskii Korpus], and from the forces stationed in Finland was formed the Separate Finland Corps [Otdelnyi Finlyandskii Korpus] (67).

12 February 1816– The 17th Jäger Regiment, for distinction, was retitled as the 7th Carabiniers; the 46th Jägers were named – the 17th Jägers, and the 57th – the 46th. Together with this the Sevastopol Infantry Regiment was transferred from the 19th Division to the 20th, and from the latter the 15th Jägers were reassigned to the 19th (68).

4 August 1816– The 4th and 34th Jägers from the 4th Infantry Division were reassigned: the first—to the 15th Division, and the second—to the 17th. To replace them in the 4th Division came: the 47th Jägers—from the 15th Division, and the 48th—from the 17th (69).

5 August 1816– Graf Arakcheev's Grenadier Regiment was designated for Military Settlement in Novgorod Province, where its 2nd Battalion went to begin settling in, having received the title of the regiment's Settled [Poselennyi] Battalion (70).

1 February 1817– There was a new distribution of forces to the Armies and Corps:

> a.) 1st Army:
> In the 1st Infantry Corps — 5th, 14th, and 25th Infantry Divisions.
> — — 2nd —————— 6th, 17th, and 28th —— ——
> — — 3rd —————— 15th and 26th —— ——
> — — 4th —————— 7th, 11th, and 24th —— ——
> — — 5th —————— 8th, 10th, and 23rd —— ——
> b.) 2nd Army:
> In the 6th Infantry Corps — 13th and 16th Infantry Divisions.
> — — 7th —————— 18th and 22nd —— ——

The 9th, 12th, 19th, 20th, and 21st Divisions, as compared with the distribution of 28 October, 1814, were unchanged, but the 27th was designated to be separate until further notice (71).

13 March 1817– The Yelets and Polotsk infantry regiments from the 11th Division were designated as part of the Corps of Settled Troops [Korpus Poselennykh voisk] (72).

21 June 1817– The Pernau Grenadier Regiment was designated for Military Settlement in Novgorod Province, where its 2nd Battalion went to begin settling in, having received the title of the regiment's Settled Battalion (73).

1 July 1817– The 4th Infantry Division was renamed the 28th, and the 28th—the 4th, and along with this the Otdelnyi Litovskii Korpus [Separate Lithuania Corps] was formed from the 27th Division and the new 28th (74).

12 July 1817– In the Separate Lithuania Corps the following regiments were reassigned:

> Lithuania Inf. and 47th and 48th Jägers, from the 28th Inf. Div. to the 27th.
> Zhitomir — — 49th — 50th — — — 27th — — — 28th (75).

26 July 1817– The following regiments were also reassigned:

> Penza Infanry and 8th Jägers, from the 23rd Inf. Div. to the 9th.
> Apsheron — — 38th — — — 9th — — — 23rd (76).

12 August 1817– The remaining regiments of the 1st Grenadier Division: His Majesty the Emperor of Austria's and His Majesty the King of Prussia's Grenadiers and the 1st and 2nd Carabiniers, were designated for Military Settlement in Novgorod Province, where their second battalions went to begin settling in, having received the title of the Settled battalions of these regiments (77).

25 September 1817– An organization list was approved for the regiments of the Separate Lithuania Corps:

> 27th Infantry Div., in the 1st Brigade: Brest and Bialystok Infantry.
> — — 2nd —— Lithuania and Vilna Infantry.
> — — 3rd —— 47th and 48th Jägers.
> 28th Infantry Div., in the 1st Brigade: Volhynia and Minsk Infantry.
> — — 2nd —— Podolia and Zhitomir Infantry.
> — — 3rd —— 49th and 50th Jägers.

With this, the other regiments in Infantry divisions were distributed as follows:

a.) 1st Army:
> 1st Infantry Corps:
> 5th Div., 1st Brigade: Perm and Sevsk Infantry.
>   2nd —— Mogilev and Prince Wilhelm of Prussia's Infantry.
>   3rd —— 23rd and 24th Jägers.
> 14th Div., 1st Brigade: Tula and Tenginsk Infantry.
>   2nd —— Navaginsk and Estonia ——.
>   3rd —— 25th and 26th Jägers.
> 25th Div., 1st Brigade: 1st and 2nd Marines.
>   2nd —— 3rd Marines and Voronezh Infantry.
>   3rd —— 31st and 14th Jägers.
> 2nd Infantry Corps:
> 6th Div., 1st Brigade: Azov and Nizovsk Infantry.
>   2nd —— Kopore and Bryansk ——.
>   3rd —— 18th and 21st Jägers.

17th Div., 1st Brigade: Ryazan and Belozersk Infantry.

         2nd — — Ladoga and Odessa — —.

         3rd — — 34th and 30th Jägers.

4th Div., 1st Brigade: Chernigov and Murom Infantry.

         2nd — — Reval and Selenginsk — —.

         3rd — — 1st and 3rd Jägers.

3rd Infantry Corps:

15th Div., 1st Brigade: Vitebsk and Kozlov Infantry.

         2nd — — Kolyvan and Kura — —.

         3rd — — 4th and 13th Jägers.

26th Div., 1st Brigade: Nizhnii-Novgorod and Poltava Infantry.

         2nd — — Kremenchug and Orel — —.

         3rd — — 5th and 42nd Jägers.

4th Infantry Corps:

7th Div., 1st Brigade: Pskov and Moscow Infantry.

         2nd — — Libau and Sofiya — —.

         3rd — — 11th and 36th Jägers.

11th Div., 1st Brigade: Yelets and Polotsk Infantry.

         2nd — — Rylsk and Yekaterinoslavl — —.

         3rd — — 33rd and 46th Jägers.

24th Div., 1st Brigade: Shirvan and Butyrskii Infantry.

         2nd — — Ufa and Tomsk — —.

         3rd — — 19th and 40th Jägers.

5th Infantry Corps:

8th Div., 1st Brigade: Archangel and Schlüsselburg Infantry.

         2nd — — Old Ingermanland and Ukraine — —.

         3rd — —37th and 7th Jägers.

10th Div., 1st Brigade: Kursk and Yaroslavl Infantry.

         2nd — — Crimea and Simbirsk — —.

         3rd — — 29th and 20th Jägers.

23rd Div., 1st Brigade: Uglich and Apsheron Infantry.

         2nd — — Borodino and Tarutino — —.

         3rd — — 35th and 38th Jägers.

b.)2nd Army:

6th Infantry Corps:

13th Div., 1st Brigade: Velikie-Luki and Saratov Infantry.

         2nd — — Galich Infantry and 4th Marines.

         3rd — — 12th and 22nd Jägers.

16th Div., 1st Brigade: Nyslott and Okhotsk Infantry.

         2nd — — Kamchatka and Mingrelia — —.

         3rd — — 43rd and 27th Jägers.

7th Infantry Corps:

18th Div., 1st Brigade: Vladimir and Tambov Infantry.

         2nd — — Dnieper and Kostroma — —.

         3rd — — 28th and 32nd Jägers.

22nd Div., 1st Brigade: Vyatka and Tobolsk Infantry.

         2nd — — Staryi-Oskol and Olonets — —.

         3rd — — 45th and 29th Jägers.

c.)Corps of Forces in France [Korpus voisk vo Frantsii]:

9th Inf. Div., 1st Brigade: Nasheburg and Ryazhsk Infantry.

         2nd — — Yakutsk and Penza — —.

         3rd — — 10th and 8th Jägers.

12th Inf. Div., 1st Brigade: Smolensk and Narva Infantry.

         2nd — — Aleksopol and New Ingermanland — —.

         3rd — — 41st and 6th Jägers.

d.)Separate Caucasus Corps [Otdelnyi Kavkazskii Korpus] :
19th Inf. Div., 1st Brigade: Suzdal and Vologda Infantry.

          2nd — — Kazan Infantry and 16th Jägers.

          3rd — — Belev Infantry and 15th Jägers.

20th Inf. Div., 1st Brigade: Troitsk and Sevastopol Infantry.

          2nd — — Tiflis and Kabarda — —.

          3rd — — 9th and 17th Jägers.

e.)Separate Finland Corps [Otdelnyi Finlyandskii Korpus]:
21st Inf. Div., 1st Brigade: Viborg and Neva Infantry.

          2nd — — Petrovsk and Villmanstrand — —.

          3rd — — 44th and 2nd Jägers (79).

24 October 1817– Villages assigned for the settlement of the Pernau Grenadier Regiment in Novgorod District [Novgorodskii uezd] were designated the Military Settlement Region of the Pernau Grenadier Regiment [Okrug Voennago Poseleniya Pernovskago Grenaderskago polka] (80).

13 November 1817– Villages assigned for the settlement of Graf Arakcheev's Grenadier Regiment in Novgorod District were designated the Military Settlement Region of Graf Arakcheev's Grenadier Regiment [Okrug Voennago Poseleniya Grenaderskago Grafa Arakcheeva polka] (81).

7 December 1817– New regiments are established in the Separate Lithuania Corps: 1st and 2nd Grenadiers and the Carabinier Regiment (82).

1 February 1818– Villages assigned for the settlement of the 1st and 2nd Carabinier Regiments in the Novgorod District were designated the Military Settlement Regions of the 1st and 2nd Carabinier Regiments [Okruga Voennago Poseleniya 1-go i 2-go Karabinernykh polkov] (83).

4 February 1818– The Polotsk Infantry Regiment was designated for Military Settlement in Mogilev Province [guberniya], Klimovetsk District [povet], in the Bobylets tract [starostvo], to where its second battalion had gone having received the title Settled, and the villages which came under the regiment's Military Settlement were designated the Military Settlement Region of the Polotsk Infantry Regiment [Okrug Voennago Poseleniya Polotskago Pekhotnago polka]. Together with this, the villages in the same tract which had been set aside under the Settled Battalion of the Yelets Infantry Regiment were named the Military Settlement Region of the Yelets Infantry Regiment [Okrug Voennago Poseleniya Yeletskago Pekhotnago polka] (84)

6 February 1818– the Kaluga Infantry Regiment was named Prince Wilhelm of Prussia's Infantry Regiment [Pekhotnyi Printsa Vilgelma Prusskago polk] (85).

13 February 1818– Villages assigned for the settlement in the Novgorod District of Grenadier Regiments: His Majesty the Emperor of Austria's and His Majesty the King of Prussia's, were designated the Military Settlement Regions of H.M. the Emperor of Austria's and H.M. the King of Prussia's Grenadier Regiments [Okruga Voennago Poseleniya Grenaderskago E.V. Imperatora Avstriiskago i Grenaderskago E.V. Korolya Prusskago polkov] (86).

20 June 1818– The Pernau Grenadier Regiment was named The Crown Prince of Prussia's Grenadier Regiment [Grenaderskii Naslednago Printsa Prusskago polk] (87).

28 August 1818– The following regiments were reassigned from one division to another:

    From the15th Division to the 16th — KolyvanInfantry.

        — — 25th — — — — — — 13th — Tomsk — — —

        — — 25th — — — — — — 15th — Voronezh — — —

        — — 6th — — — — — 24th — Nizovsk — — —

        — — 21st — — — — — — 6th — Neva — — —

        — — 16th — — — — — 21st — Nyslott — — —

        — — 13th — — — — — 25th — 4th Marines (88).

25 January 1819– The following regiments, belonging to the 9th and 12th infantry divisions stationed in France, were transferred to other divisions:

    From the 9th Division — Ryazhsk Infantry, to the 10th.

                Yakutsk — — — — 16th.

                Penza — — — — 15th.

                10th Jägers — — 17th.

                8th — — — — 17th.

    From the 12th Division — Smolensk Infantry, to the 7th.

                Narva — — — — 6th.

                Aleksopol — — — — 26th.

                Novoingermanland — — 14th.

                26th Jägers — — 14th.

To replace these regiments came:

To the 9th Division — Shirvan Infantry, from the 10th.

     Kura — — — — 15th.

     Mingrelia — — — — 16th.

     43rd Jägers — — 16th.

     45th — — — — 22nd.

To the 12th Division — Nizhnii-Novgorod Infantry, from the 26th.

     Apsheron — — — — 23rd.

     Tenginsk — — — — 14th.

     Navaginsk — — — — 14th.

     42nd Jägers — — 26th.

The Nasheburg Infantry Regiment remained, as before, in the 9th Infantry Division, and the 41st Jägers—in the 12th. Thus the regiments of these divisions had achieved the following distribution:

  9th Infantry Div., 1st Brigade: — Nasheburg and Shirvan Infantry.

      2nd — — — Kura and Mingrelia Infantry.

      3rd — — — 43rd and 45th Jägers.

  12th — — — — 1st — — — Nizhnii-Novgorod and Apsheron Infantry.

      2nd — — — Tenginsk and Navaginsk Infantry.

      3rd — — — 41st and 42nd Jägers.

Along with this, consequent to the return to Russia of the troops which had been in France, the 9th Division was assigned to the 7th Infantry Corps, and the 12th—to the 3rd (89).

28 February 1819– The second battalions of the Pskov, Old Ingermanland, New Ingermanland, and Velikie-Luki Infantry, the 1st, 2nd, 3rd, and 4th Marines, and the 5th, 6th, 1st, and 2nd Jägers, were assigned to the Corps of Settled Troops [Korpus Poselennykh voisk] (90).

2 July 1819– The following regiments were transferred to other divisions:

  From the 12th Division — Apsheron Infantry, to the 20th.

      Tenginsk — — — — 19th.

      Navaginsk — — — — 19th.

      41st and 42nd Jägers — — 20th.

  — — — 9th — — — — Shirvan Infantry, to the 20th.

      Kura — — — — 20th.

      Mingrelia — — — — 19th.

      43rd and 45th Jägers — — 19th.

In exchange for these regiments, from the 19th and 20th Infantry Divisions went:

  From the 19th Division — Suzdal Infantry, to the 18th.

      Vologda — — — — 4th.

      Kazan — — — — 18th.

      Belev — — — — 10th.

      15th and 16th Jägers — — 15th.

  — — — 20th — — — Troitsk Infantry, to the 15th.

      Sevastopol — — — — 9th.

      9th Jägers — — 17th.

      17th — — — — 26th.

After these transfers, the regiments of the 19th and 20th Infantry Divisions received the following assignments:

  19th Infantry Div., 1st Brigade: — Kabarda and Tenginsk Infantry.

      2nd — — — Navaginsk and Mingrelia Infantry.

      3rd — — — 43rd and 45th Jägers.

  20th — — — — 1st — — — Apsheron and Tiflis Infantry.

      2nd — — — Shirvan and Kura Infantry.

      3rd — — — 41st and 42nd Jägers (91).

16 July 1819– The 44th Jäger Regiment was renamed the 45th, and the 45th became the 44th (92).

23 July 1819– The second battalions of: the Neva, Sofiya, Narva, Kopore, Belozersk, Olonets, Schlüsselburg, Ladoga, Smolensk, Mogilev, Vitebsk, Kursk, Staryi-Oskol, Rylsk, Voronezh, Murom, Nizhnii-Novgorod, Nizovsk, Simbirsk, Penza, Chernigov, Poltava, Aleksopol, and Kremenchug Infantry; the 11th, 12th, 10th, 19th, 20th, 23rd, 24th, 13th, 14th, and 18th Jägers; as well as of the Suzdal, Vologda, Belev, and Troitsk Infantry and the 15th, 16th, 9th, and 17th Jägers, transferred on 2 July from the 19th

Division to the 20th, were all assigned to the Corps of Settled Troops (93).

18 October 1819– The regiments of Army infantry were distributed as follows:

a.)1st Army:

Grenadier Corps:

    2nd Grenadier Div., 1st Brigade: Kiev and Taurica Grenadiers.

                        2nd — — Yekaterinoslavl and Moscow Grenadiers.

                        3rd — — 3rd and 4th Carabiniers.

      3rd — — — — — 1st — — Siberia and Little Russia Grenadiers.

                        2nd — — Phanagoria and Astrakhan Grenadiers.

                        3rd — — 5th and 6th Carabiniers.

1st Infantry Corps:

    5th Division, 1st Brigade: Perm and Mogilev Infantry.

                        2nd — — Prince Wilhelm of Prussia's and Estonia Infantry.

                        3rd — — 23rd and 24th Jägers.

    14th — — — 1st Brigade: Pskov and Old Ingermanland Infantry.

                        2nd — — New Ingermanland and Velikie-Luki Infantry.

                        3rd — — 6th and 26th Jägers.

    25th — — — 1st Brigade: 1st and 2nd Marines.

                        2nd — — 3rd and 4th — —

                        3rd — — 2nd and 14th Jägers.

2nd Infantry Corps:

    4th Division, 1st Brigade: Chernigov and Reval Infantry.

                        2nd — — Kostroma and Galich — —

                        3rd — — 1st and 3rd Jägers.

    6th — — — 1st Brigade: Azov and Narva Infantry.

                        2nd — — Neva and Kopore — —

                        3rd — — 8th and 21st Jägers.

    17th — — — 1st Brigade: Schlüsselburg and Belozersk Infantry.

                        2nd — — Ladoga and Odessa — —

                        3rd — — 9th and 10th Jägers.

3rd Infantry Corps:

    12th Division, 1st Brigade: Murom and Nizhnii-Novgorod Infantry.

                        2nd — — Simbirsk and Uglich — —

                        3rd — — 4th and 13th Jägers.

    15th — — — 1st Brigade: Troitsk and Tambov Infantry.

                        2nd — — Penza and Vologda — —

                        3rd — — 15th and 16th Jägers.

    26th — — — 1st Brigade: Aleksopol and Poltava Infantry.

                        2nd — — Kremenchug and Orel — —

                        3rd — — 5th and 18th Jägers.

4th Infantry Corps:

    7th Division, 1st Brigade: Smolensk and Vitebsk Infantry.

                        2nd — — Libau and Sofiya — —

                        3rd — — 11th and 20th Jägers.

    11th — — — 1st Brigade: Yelets and Polotsk Infantry.

                        2nd — — Sevsk and Bryansk — —

                        3rd — — 33rd and 22nd Jägers.

    24th — — — 1st Brigade: Nizovsk and Kursk Infantry.

                        2nd — — Rylsk and Voronezh — —

                        3rd — — 19th and 40th Jägers.

5th Infantry Corps:

    8th Division, 1st Brigade: Archangel and Suzdal Infantry.

                        2nd — — Yaroslavl and Ukraine — —

                        3rd — — 7th and 25th Jägers.

10th ——— 1st Brigade: Ryazan and Ryazhsk Infantry.
           2nd —— Belev and Tula ——
           3rd —— 29th and 30th Jägers.
23rd ——— 1st Brigade: Moscow and Butyrskii Infantry.
           2nd —— Borodino and Tarutino ——
           3rd —— 35th and 28th Jägers.

b.)2nd Army:

6th Infantry Corps:
13th Division, 1st Brigade: Yekaterinburg and Tomsk Infantry.
           2nd —— Kolyvan and Saratov ——
           3rd —— 12th and 31st Jägers.
16th ——— 1st Brigade: Selenginsk and Yakutsk Infantry.
           2nd —— Okhotsk and Kamchatka ——
           3rd —— 34th and 27th Jägers.
7th Infantry Corps:
18th Division, 1st Brigade: Kazan and Vladimir Infantry.
           2nd —— Vyatka and Ufa ——
           3rd —— 36th and 32nd Jägers.
22nd ——— 1st Brigade: Tobolsk and Staryi-Oskol Infantry.
           2nd —— Dnieper and Olonets ——
           3rd —— 37th and 38th Jägers.
9th ——— 1st Brigade: Nasheburg and Sevastopol Infantry.
           2nd —— Crimea and Kozlov ——
           3rd —— 39th and 17th Jägers.

c.)Separate Georgia Corps [Otdelnyi Gruzinskii Korpus] :

Reserve Grenadier Brig.: Kherson and Georgia Grenadiers and 7th Carabiniers.
19th Infantry Division, 1st Brigade: Kabarda and Tenginsk Infantry.
           2nd —— Navaginsk and Mingrelia ——
           3rd —— 43rd and 45th Jägers.
20th ——— ——— 1st Brigade: Apsheron and Tiflis Infantry.
           2nd —— Shirvan and Kura ——
           3rd —— 41st and 42nd Jägers.

d.)Separate Finland Corps[Otdelnyi Finlyandskii Korpus]:

21st Infantry Division, 1st Brigade: Viborg and Nyslott Infantry.
           2nd —— Petrovsk and Villmanstrand ——
           3rd —— 44th and 46th Jägers.

e.)Separate Lithuania Corps [Otdelnyi Litovskii Korpus] :

27th Infantry Division, 1st Brigade: Brest and Bialystok Infantry.
           2nd —— Lithuania and Vilna ——
           3rd —— 47th and 48th Jägers.
28th ——— ——— 1st Brigade: Volhynia and Minsk Infantry.
           2nd —— Podolia and Zhitomir ——
           3rd —— 49th and 50th Jägers.

The regiments of the 1st Grenadier Division, as before, belonged to the Guards Corps (94).

8 December 1819– The 26th Jäger Regiment was renamed the 35th, and the 35th—the 26th (95).

13 January 1820– The second battalions of the Kostroma, Galich, Archangel, Yaroslavl, Ugilch, Ryazan, Ryazhsk, Tula, Vladimir, Moscow, Butyrskii, and Borodino Infantry, and the 7th, 8th, 25th, 26th, 27th, 28th, 29th, and 30th Jägers—were assigned to the Corps of Settled Troops (96).

20 May 1820– Infantry divisions are directed to be named:

a.) First Army:

1st Infantry Corps, 25th Division — 1st.
           5th ———— 2nd.
           14th ———— 3rd.
2nd ——— —— 4th ———— 4th.
           17th ———— 5th.
           6th ———— 6th.

3rd ——— —— 12th ———— 7th.
                            15th ———— 8th.
                            26th ———— 9th.
4th ——— —— 7th ———— 10th.
                            11th ———— 11th.
                            24th ———— 12th.
5th ——— —— 8th ———— 13th.
                            23rd ———— 14th.
                            10th ———— 15th.

b.) Second Army:

6th Infantry Corps, 16th Division — 16th.
                            13th ———— 17th.
7th ——— —— 18th ————18th.
                            22nd ———— 19th.
                            9th ———— 20th.

c.) Separate Georgia Corps:20th Division—21st.
                          19th ——— 22nd.
d.) ——— Finland ——— 21st ———— 23rd.
e.)——— Lithuania ———27th ———— 24th.
                          28th ———— 25th.
f.) ——— Orenburg ——— 29th ———— 26th.
g.)——— Siberia ——— 30th ———— 27th.

After this renumbering of divisions, the distribution of regiments to them was as follows:

1st Division, 1st Brigade: 1st and 2nd Marines.
                        2nd —— 3rd and 4th ——
                        3rd —— 1st and 2nd Jägers.
2nd ——— 1st —— Prince Wilhelm of Prussia's and Libau Infantry.
                     2nd —— Reval and Estonia Infantry.
                     3rd —— 3rd and 4th Jägers.
3rd ——— 1st —— Old Ingermanland and New Ingermanland Infantry.
                     2nd —— Pskov and Velikie-Luki Infantry.
                     3rd —— 5th and 6th Jägers.
4th ——— 1st —— Archangel and Vologda Infantry.
                     2nd —— Kostroma and Galich ——
                     3rd —— 7th and 8th Jägers.
5th ——— 1st —— Belozersk and Olonets Infantry.
                     2nd —— Schlüsselburg and Ladoga ——
                     3rd —— 9th and 10th Jägers.
6th ——— 1st —— Neva and Sofiya Infantry.
                     2nd —— Narva and Kopore ——
                     3rd ——11th and 12th Jägers.
7th ——— 1st —— Murom and Nizhnii-Novgorod Infantry.
                     2nd —— Nizovsk and Simbirsk ——
                     3rd —— 13th and 14th Jägers.
8th ——— 1st —— Troitsk and Penza Infantry.
                     2nd —— Tambov and Saratov ——
                     3rd —— 15th and 16th Jägers.
9th ——— 1st —— Chernigov and Poltava Infantry.
                     2nd ——Aleksopol and Kremenchug ——
                     3rd ——17th and 18th Jägers.
10th ——— 1st —— Smolensk and Mogilev Infantry.
                     2nd —— Vitebsk and Polotsk ——
                     3rd —— 19th and 20th Jägers.
11th ——— 1st —— Yelets and Sevsk Infantry.
                     2nd —— Bryansk and Orel ——
                     3rd —— 21st and 22nd Jägers.

12th ——— 1st —— Kursk and Staryi-Oskol Infantry.
              2nd —— Rylsk and Voronezh ——
              3rd —— 23rd and 24th Jägers.
13th ——— 1st —— Vladimir and Suzdal Infantry.
              2nd —— Uglich and Yaroslavl ——
              3rd —— 25th and 26th Jägers.
14th ——— 1st —— Moscow and Butyrskii Infantry.
              2nd —— Borodino and Tarutino ——
              3rd —— 27th and 28th Jägers.
15th ——— 1st —— Ryazan and Ryazhsk Infantry.
              2nd —— Belev and Tula ——
              3rd —— 29th and 30th Jägers.
16th ——— 1st —— Selenginsk and Yakutsk Infantry.
              2nd —— Okhotsk and Kamchatka ——
              3rd —— 31st and 32nd Jägers.
17th ——— 1st —— Yekaterinburg and Tobolsk Infantry.
              2nd —— Tomsk and Kolyvan ——
              3rd —— 33rd and 34th Jägers.
18th ——— 1st —— Kazan and Vyatka Infantry.
              2nd —— Ufa and Perm ——
              3rd —— 35th and 36th Jägers.
19th ——— 1st —— Azov and Dnieper Infantry.
              2nd —— Ukraine and Odessa ——
              3rd —— 37th and 38th Jägers.
20th ——— 1st —— Crimea and Sevastopol Infantry.
              2nd —— Kozlov and Nasheburg ——
              3rd —— 39th and 40th Jägers.
21st ——— 1st —— Kura and Apsheron Infantry.
              2nd —— Tiflis and Shirvan ——
              3rd —— 41st and 42nd Jägers.
22nd ——— 1st —— Tenginsk and Navaginsk Infantry.
              2nd —— Kabarda Infantry and 43rd Jägers.
              3rd —— Mingrelia Infantry and 44th Jägers.
23rd ——— 1st —— Brigade: Viborg and Nyslott Infantry.
              2nd —— Petrovsk and Villmanstrand ——
              3rd —— 45th and 46th Jägers.
24th ——— 1st —— Brest and Bialystok Infantry.
              2nd —— Lithuanian and Vilna ——
              3rd —— 47th and 48th Jägers.
25th ——— 1st —— Volhynia and Minsk Infantry.
              2nd —— Podolia and Zhitomir ——
              3rd —— 49th and 50th Jägers (97).

From the divisions listed here, the second battalions of the 1st, 3rd, 4th, 5th, 6th, 7th, 8th, 9th, 10th, 12th, 13th, 14th, and 15th Divisions, and the Yelets Infantry Regiment from the 11th Division, were in the Corps of Settled Troops, where from the Army infantry there were also the second battalions of the regiments of the 1st Grenadier Division (98).

29 May 1820– The second battalions of the 11th Infantry Division's regiments: the Sevsk, Bryansk, and Orel Infantry and the 21st and 23rd Jägers, were assigned to the Corps of Settled Troops (99).

11 October 1820– The Separate Georgia Corps was renamed the Separate Caucasus Corps [Otdelnyi Kavkazskii Korpus] (100).

3 February 1821– The Corps of Settled Troops received the designation Separate Corps of Military Settlements [Otdelnyi Korpus Voennykh Poselenii] (101).

12 July 1821– The second battalions of the 2nd Infantry Division's regiments: Prince Wilhelm of Prussia's, Libau, Reval, and Estonia Infantry, and the 3rd and 4th Jägers, were assigned to the Separate Corps of Military Settlements [Otdelnyi Korpus Voennykh Poselenii] (102).

23 October 1822– The Libau Infantry Regiment was named Prince Karl of Prussia's Infantry Regiment [Pekhotnyi Printsa Karla Prusskago polk] (103).

8 February 1824– The second battalions of the 2nd and 3rd Grenadier Divisions' regiments: the Kiev, Taurica, Yekaterinoslavl,

Moscow, Siberia, Little Russia, Phanagoria, and Astrakhan Grenadiers and the 3rd, 4th, 5th, and 6th Carabiniers, were designated to form a special detachment in the Separate Corps of Military Settlement called the Staraya Russa [Starorusskii] (104).

15 February 1824– The second battalions of the regiments of the 16th, 18th, and 19th Infantry Divisions: the Selenginsk, Yakutsk, Okhotsk, Kamchatka, Kazan, Vyatka, Ufa, Perm, Azov, Dnieper, Ukraine, and Odessa Infantry and the 31st, 32nd, 35th, 36th, 37th, and 38th Jägers, were assigned to the Separate Corps of Military Settlements (105).

26 February 1824– The second battalions of the 2nd and 3rd Grenadier Divisions' regiments were named their Settled [Poselenyi] battalions, and the villages in the Staraya-Russa District designated for the installation of these regiments were called the Military Settlement Districts [Okruga] of the Kiev, Taurica, Yekaterinoslavl, Moscow, Siberia, Little Russia, Phanagoria, and Astrakhan Grenadier Regiments and the 3rd, 4th, 5th, and 6th Carabiniers (106).

3 March 1824– In the regiments of the 1st Grenadier Division: His Majesty the Emperor of Austria's, His Majesty the King of Prussia's, The Crown Prince of Prussia's, and Graf Arakcheev's Grenadier Regiments, and the 1st and 2nd Carabiniers, their second, i.e. Settled, battalions were ordered to be numbered 3rd, and the previous active-duty third battalions were to be called second active battalions. Consequent to this the companies of these battalions were also renumbered: the second Grenadier companies—as third, and third Grenadier companies—as second; the seventh, eighth, and ninth Fusilier companies became the fourth, fifth, and sixth Fusiliers, and vice versa (107).

26 March 1824– The renumbering of second battalions as third, and third battalions as second, was extended to the regiments of the 2nd and 3rd Grenadier Divisions, and also to all those Infantry regiments which had second battalions assigned to the Separate Corps of Military Settlements (108).

10 July 1824– A 4th battalion was established for Graf Arakcheev's Regiment, consisting of four companies: the 4th Grenadier and the 10th, 11th, and 12th Fusilier (109).

4 March 1825– The following regiments of the Separate Lithuania Corps were renamed: the 1st Grenadiers—as the Samogitia Grenadiers [Samogitskii Grenaderskii], the 2nd Grenadiers—as the Lutsk Grenadiers [Lutskii Grenaderskii], and the Carabiniers—as the Nesvizh Carabiniers [Nesvizhskii Karabinernyi]. With this, on the day that Emperor Alexander I passed away, 19 November, 1825, the entire force of Army infantry was as follows:

a.) In the 1st Army:

Grenadier Corps:

2nd Grenadier Div., 1st Brigade: Kiev and Taurica Grenadiers.

2nd — — Yekaterinoslavl and Moscow Grenadiers.

3rd — — 3rd and 4th Carabiniers.

3rd Grenadier Div., 1st — — Siberia and Little Russia Grenadiers.

2nd — — Phanagoria and Astrakhan Grenadiers.

3rd — — 5th and 6th Carabiniers.

1st Infantry Corps:

1st Inf. Division, 1st Brigade: 1st Marine Regiment.

2nd — — — — —

2nd — — 3rd — — — — —

4th — — — — —

3rd — — 1st Jäger Regiment.

2nd — — — — —

2nd Inf. Division, 1st — — Prince Wilhelm of Prussia's Infantry.

Prince Karl of Prussia's Infantry.

2nd — — Reval Infantry.

Estonia — — —

3rd — — 3rd Jägers.

4th — —

3rd Inf. Division, 1st — — Old Ingermanland Infantry.

New Ingermanland — — —

2nd — — Pskov — — —

Velikie-Luki — — —

3rd — — 5th Jägers.

6th — —

2nd Infantry Corps:

4th Inf. Division, 1st Brigade: Archangel Infantry.

Vologda — — —

2nd — — Kostroma — — —

Galich — — —

```
                3rd  —— 7th Jägers.
                         8th ——
5th Inf. Division, 1st —— Belozersk Infantry.
                         Olonets ———
                2nd —— Schlüsselburg ———
                         Ladoga ———
                3rd  —— 9th Jägers.
                         10th ——
6th Inf. Division, 1st —— Neva Infantry.
                         Sofiya ———
                2nd —— Narva ———
                         Kopore ———
                3rd —— 11th Jägers.
                         12th ——
3rd Infantry Corps:
  7th Inf. Division, 1st Brigade: Murom Infantry.
                           Nizhnii-Novgorod ———
                2nd  —— Nizovsk ———
                           Simbirsk ———
                3rd  —— 13th Jägers.
                           14th ——
8th Inf. Division, 1st —— Troitsk Infantry.
                           Penza ———
                2nd ——Tambov ———
                           Saratov ———
                3rd ——15th Jägers.
                           16th ——
9th Inf. Division, 1st —— Chernigov Infantry.
                           Poltava ———
                2nd —— Aleksopol ———
                           Kremenchug ———
                3rd —— 17th Jägers.
                           18th ——
4th Infantry Corps:
  10th Inf. Division, 1st Brigade: Smolensk Infantry.
                             Mogilev ———
                2nd  —— Vitebsk Infantry.
                             Polotsk ———
                3rd  —— 19th Jägers.
                             20th ——
11th Inf. Division, 1st —— Yelets Infantry.
                             Sevsk ———
                2nd —— Bryansk ———
                             Orel ———
                3rd —— 21st Jägers.
                             22nd ——
12th Inf. Division, 1st —— Kursk Infantry.
                             Staryi-Oskol ———
                2nd —— Rylsk ———
                             Voronezh ———
                3rd —— 23rd Jägers.
                             24th ——
5th Infantry Corps:
  13th Inf. Division, 1st Brigade: Vladimir Infantry.
                             Suzdal ———
                2nd  —— Uglich ———
```

```
                        Yaroslavl ———
          3rd    —— 25th Jägers.
                        26th ——
14th Inf. Division, 1st  —— Moscow Infantry.
                        Butyrskii ———
          2nd   —— Borodino ———
                        Tarutino ———
          3rd    —— 27th Jägers.
                        28th ——
15th Inf. Division, 1st —— Ryazan Infantry.
                        Ryazhsk ———
          2nd   —— Belev ———
                        Tula ———
          3rd    —— 29th Jägers.
                        30th ——
```

b.)In the 2nd Army:

6th Infantry Corps:

```
16th Inf. Division, 1st Brigade: Selenginsk Infantry.
                             Yakutsk ———
          2nd    —— Okhotsk ———
                             Kamchatka ———
          3rd    —— 31st Jägers.
                             32nd ——
17th Inf. Division, 1st   —— Yekaterinburg Infantry.
                             Tobolsk ———
          2nd   —— Tomsk ———
                             Kolyvan ———
          3rd   —— 33rd Jägers.
                             34th ——
```

7th Infantry Corps:

```
18th Inf. Division, 1st Brigade: Kazan Infantry.
                             Vyatka ———
          2nd    —— Ufa ———
                             Perm ———
          3rd    —— 35th Jägers.
                             36th ——
19th Inf. Division, 1st    —— Azov Infantry.
                             Dnieper ———
          2nd    —— Ukraine ———
                             Odessa ———
          3rd    —— 37th Jägers.
                             38th ——
20th Inf. Division, 1st    —— Crimea Infantry.
                             Sevastopol ———
          2nd   —— Kozlov ———
                             Nasheburg ———
          3rd    —— 39th Jägers.
                             40th ——
```

The third battalions of all these regiments, except those in the 17th and 20th Divisions, were in the Separate Corps of Military Settlements.

c.)In the Separate Georgia Corps:

Reserve Grenadier Brig: Kherson and Georgia Grenadiers and 7th Carabiniers.

```
21st Inf. Division, 1st Brigade: Kura and Apsheron Infantry.
          2nd    —— Tiflis and Shirvan ——
          3rd    —— 41st and 42nd Jägers.
```

22nd — — — — 1st — — Tenginsk and Navaginsk Infantry.
                          2nd — — Kabarda Infantry and 43rd Jägers.
                          3rd — — Mingrelia Infantry and 44th Jägers.

d.)In the Separate Finland Corps:

23rd Inf. Division, 1st Brigade: Viborg and Nyslott Infantry.
                    2nd — — Petrovsk and Villmanstrand — —
                       3rd — — 45th and 46th Jägers.

e.)In the Separate Lithuania Corps:

24th Inf. Division, 1st Brigade: Brest and Bialystok Infantry.
                    2nd — — Lithuanian and Vilna — —
                       3rd — — 47th and 48th Jägers.
25th — — — 1st — — Volhynia and Minsk Infantry.
                       2nd — — Podolia and Zhitomir — —
                       3rd — — 49th and 50th Jägers.

With this corps there were also the Samogitia and Lutsk Grenadiers and the Nesvizh Carabiniers, which together with the Lithuania and Volhynia Regiments of the Life-Guards and the Polish Grenadiers made up the 1st, 2nd, and 3rd Brigades of the Combined Guards Grenadier Division [Svodnaya Gvardeiskaya Grenaderskaya diviziya].

     f.) In the Separate Corps of Military Settlements:

FIRST, SECOND AND THIRD BATTALIONS:

1st Grenadier Division, — His Majesty the Emperor of Austria's, His Majesty the King of Prussia's, The Crown Prince of Prussia's, and Graf Arakcheev's, and the 1st and 2nd Carabiniers. (In the Novgorod settlement.)

THIRD BATTALIONS OF THE REGIMENTS:

2nd Grenadier Division, — Kiev, Taurica, Moscow, and Yekaterinburg Grenadiers, and 3rd and 4th Carabiniers.
(In the Novgorod settlement.)
3rd Grenadier Division, — Siberia, Little Russia, Astrakhan, and Phanagoria Grenadiers, and 5th and 6th Carabiniers.
(In the Novgorod settlement.)
1st Infantry Division, — 1st, 2nd, 3rd, and 4th Marines, and 1st and 2nd Jägers.
(In the Novgorod settlement.)
2nd Infantry Division, — Prince Wilhelm of Prussia's, Prince Karl of Prussia's, Reval, and Estonia Infantry, and 3rd and 4th Jägers.
(In the Novgorod settlement.)
3rd Infantry Division, — Old Ingermanland, New Ingermanland, Pskov, and Velikie-Luki Infantry, and 5th and 6th Jägers.
(In the Novgorod settlement.)
4th Infantry Division, — Archangel, Vologda, Kostroma, and Galich Infantry, and 7th and 8th Jägers.
(In the Novgorod settlement.)
5th Infantry Division, — Belozersk, Olonets, Schlüsselburg, and Ladoga Infantry, and 9th and 10th Jägers.
(In the Novgorod settlement.)
6th Infantry Division, — Neva, Sofiya, Narva, and Kopore Infantry, and 11th and 12th Jägers.
(In the Novgorod settlement.)
7th Infantry Division, — Murom, Nizhnii-Novgorod, Nizovsk, and Simbirsk Infantry, and 13th and 14th Jägers.
(In the Novgorod settlement.)
8th Infantry Division, — Troitsk, Penza, Tambov, and Saratov Infantry, and 15th and 16th Jägers.
(In the Novgorod settlement.)
9th Infantry Division, — Chernigov, Poltava, Aleksopol, and Kremenchug Infantry, and 17th and 18th Jägers.
(In the Novgorod settlement.)
10th Infantry Division, — Smolensk, Mogilev, Vitebsk, and Polotsk Infantry, and 19th and 20th Jägers.
(In the Mogilev settlement.)
11th Infantry Division, — Yelets, Sevsk, Bryansk, and Orel Infantry, and 21st and 22nd Jägers.
(In the Mogilev settlement.)
12th Infantry Division, — Kursk, Staryi-Oskol, Rylsk, and Voronezh Infantry, and 23rd and 24th Jägers.
(In the Novgorod settlement.)
13th Infantry Division, — Vladimir, Suzdal, Uglich and Yaroslavl Infantry, and 25th and 26th Jägers.
(In the Slobodsko-Ukraina settlement.)
14th Infantry Division, — Moscow, Butyrskii, Borodino, and Tarutino Infantry, and 27th and 28th Jägers.
(In the Slobodsko-Ukraina settlement.)

15th Infantry Division — Ryazan, Ryazhsk, Belev, and Tula Infantry, and 29th and 30th Jägers. (In the Slobodsko-Ukraina settlement.)

16th Infantry Division, — Selenginsk, Yakutsk, Okhotsk, and Kamchatka Infantry, and 31st and 32nd Jägers. (In the Kherson settlement.)

18th Infantry Division, — Kazan, Vyatka, Ufa, and Perm Infantry, and 35th and 36th Jägers. (In the Kherson settlement.)

19th Infantry Division, — Azov, Dnieper, Ukraine, and Odessa Infantry, and 37th and 38th Jägers (In the Kherson settlement.)(110).

NOTES

(56) PSZ, Vol. XXXII, pg. 535, No. 25,352.
(57) Highest confirmed report of the Minister of Military Forces [Ministr Voennykh Sil], 16 March, 1813.
(58) PSZ, Vol. XXXII, pg. 555, No. 25,370.
(59) PSZ, Vol. XXXII, pg. 595, No. 25,420.
(60) PSZ, Vol. XXXII, pg. 660, No. 25,472.
(61) Highest Order.
(62) Highest confirmed List of forces, 29 August, 1814.
(63) Highest Order.
(64) PSZ, Vol. XXXII, pg. 1,077, No. 25,723, and List of forces for 1814.
(65) Highest Order.
(66) List of forces for 1815.
(67) Highest Order.
(68) Highest Order.
(69) PSZ, Vol. XXXIII, pg. 973, No26,385.
(70) PSZ, Vol. XXXIII, pg. 974, No. 26,389, and List of forces for 1816.
(71) List of forces for 1817.
(72) List of forces for 1817.
(73) Report of General of Artillery Graf Arakcheev to the Novgorod Civil Governor, 21 June, 1817.
(74) PSZ, Vol. XXXIV, pg. 439, No. 26,950.
(75) PSZ, Vol. XXXIV, pg. 446, No. 26,964.
(76) PSZ, Vol. XXXIV, pg. 458, No. 26,976.
(77) Report of General of Artillery Graf Arakcheev to the Novgorod Civil Governor, 12 August, 1817.
(78) PSZ, Vol. XXXIV, pg. 780, No. 27,066.
(79) List of forces for 1818.
(80) Highest Charter [Gramota] to the Pernau Grenadier Regiment and the settlers designated for its region, from 24 October, 1817.
(81) Highest Charter to the Graf Arakcheev's Grenadier Regiment.
(82) Highest Order.
(83) Highest Charter to the 1st and 2nd Carabinier Regiments and the settlers designated for their Regions, 1 February, 1818.
(84) Highest Charter to the Polotsk and Yelets Infantry Regiments and the settlers designated for their Regions, 4 February, 1818.
(85) Highest Order.
(86) Highest Charter to the Grenadier regiments: H.M. the Emperor of Austria's and H.M. the King of Prussia's, and the settlers designated for their Regions, 13 February, 1818.
(87) Highest Order.
(88) Collection of Laws and Directives relating to the area of Military Administration, 1818, Book III, pg. 175.
(89) List of forces for 1819.
(90) Order to the Settled forces, commands of G. M. Knyazhnin 2nd, 28 February, 1819, No. 25.
(91) List of forces for 1819.
(92) Highest Order.

(93) Report of the Chief of HIS IMPERIAL MAJESTY'S Headquarters to the Commander-in-Chief of the 1st Army, from 23 July, 1819, No. 1,340, and List of the Corps of Settled Forces, for 1819.

(94) List of forces for 1819.

(95) Highest Order.

(96) PSZ, Vol. XXXVII, pg. 15, No. 28,095.

(97) PSZ, Vol. XXXVII, pg. 207, No28,095, No28,276.

(98) Ibid.

(99) PSZ, Vol. XXXVII, pg. 247, No. 28,292.

(100) PSZ, Vol. XXXVII, pg. 460, No. 28,438.

(101) Order to the Separate Corps of Military Settlements, 1821, No. No14 and 15.

(102) Order to the Separate Corps of Military Settlements, from 12 July, 1821, No. 166.

(103) Highest Order.

(104) Order to the Separate Corps of Military Settlements, 8 February, 1824, No. 45.

(105) Order to the Separate Corps of Military Settlements, 15 February, 1824, No. 54.

(106) Order to the Separate Corps of Military Settlements, 26 February, 1824, No. 95.

(107) Order to the Separate Corps of Military Settlements, 3 March, 1824, No. 82.

(108) Order to the Separate Corps of Military Settlements, 26 March, 1824, No. 109.

(109) Order to the Settled infantry of the Separate Corps of Military Settlements, 10 July, 1824, No 235.

(110) Highest Order.

Czar's Guard capture 4th line regiment's standard at Austerlitz in 1805 by Willewalde (1884)

Russian Army: Musketeers, Jägers, Marines, and Carabiniers 1801-1825

CHANGES IN THE CLOTHING AND WEAPONS OF ARMY INFANTRY FROM 1801 TO 1825.

II. Musketeer Regiments.
III.Marine Regiments.
IV.Jäger Regiments.
V.Grenadier Jäger, or Carabinier, Regiments.
Notes by the translator.
Source notes.

II. MUSKETEERS REGIMENTS

The following directives, described above in regard to the uniform and armament of Grenadier regiments, were extended with equal force to Musketeer regiments: **9 April 1801** — about shortening queues; **21 June** — about generals and field and company-grade officers of the St.-Petersburg garrison wearing new-pattern hats; **15 January and 17 March 1802** — in regard to the pattern, tailoring, and colors of coats; and **30 April 1802** — about coats, accouterments, and firearm items. The only difference was that in these last subjects all combatant lower ranks of Musketeer battalions and regimental drummers wore tricorn hats [*treugolnyya shlyapy*] instead of caps [*shapki*]. These hats were similar in all respects to those which at that time were given to noncombatants in Grenadier regiments, except with the addition of a cockade, two tassels at the corners, and one pompon above the cockade (Illus. 1344). For privates these pompons were colored according to the assignments set forth below, and those of noncommissioned officer ranks were white with a mix of black and orange (750).

6 July 1802 [sic, should be June — M.C.] — Confirmation is given to a listing of colors for pompons on grenadier caps and musketeer hats (751), based on which the colors for the above directive of 17 March and table of 30 April, which served to distinguish one Musketeer regiment from another, were as follows:

Velikie-Luki Regiment of the Finland Inspectorate:
Yellow collar and cuffs; red shoulder straps; grendier caps with yellow crowns and red bands; pompons on grenadier caps and hats: in the 1st battalion - white with a red center; in the 2nd - yellow with a red center; in the 3rd - red; drumsticks and shafts of halberds and spontoons - black (Illus. 1344).

Neva Regiment of the same Inspectorate:
Yellow collar and cuffs; white shoulder straps; grenadier caps with yellow crowns and white bands; pompons on grenadier caps and hats: in the 1st battalion - white with a yellow center; in the 2nd - yellow; in the 3rd - red with a yellow center; drumsticks and shafts of halberds and spontoons - black.

Ryazan Regiment of the same Inspectorate:
Yellow collar, cuffs, and shoulder straps; grenadier caps with yellow crowns and bands; pompons on grenadier caps and hats: in the 1st battalion - white; in the 2nd - yellow with a white center; in the 3rd - red with a white center; drumsticks and shafts of halberds and spontoons - white

Yelets Regiment of the St.-Petersburg Inspectorate:
Red collar and cuffs; yellow shoulder straps; grenadier caps with red crowns and yellow bands; pompons on grenadier caps and hats: in the 1st battalion - white with a turquiose center; in the 2nd - yellow with a turquoise center; in the 3rd - red with a turquoise center; drumsticks and shafts of halberds and spontoons - black (Illus. 1345).

Kexholm Regiment of the same Inspectorate:
Red collar and cuffs; light-raspberry shoulder straps; grenadier caps with red crowns and light-raspberry bands; pompons on grenadier caps and hats: in the 1st battalion - white with a yellow center; in the 2nd - yellow; in the 3rd - red with a yellow center; drumsticks and shafts of halberds and spontoons - coffee colored.

Belozersk Regiment of the same Inspectorate:

Red collar and cuffs; turquoise shoulder straps; grenadier caps with red crowns and turquoise bands; pompons on grenadier caps and hats: in the 1st battalion - white with a light-green center; in the 2nd - yellow with a light-green center; in the 3rd - red with a light-green center; drumsticks and shafts of halberds and spontoons - black.

Tenginsk Regiment of the same Inspectorate:

Red collar and cuffs; rose shoulder straps; grenadier caps with red crowns and rose bands; pompons on grenadier caps and hats: in the 1st battalion - white with a rose center; in the 2nd - yellow with a rose center; in the 3rd - red with a rose center; drumsticks and shafts of halberds and spontoons - coffee colored.

Lithuania Regiment of the same Inspectorate:

Red collar and cuffs; light-green shoulder straps; grenadier caps with red crowns and light-green bands; pompons on grenadier caps and hats: in the 1st battalion - white with a light-green center; in the 2nd - yellow with a light-green center; in the 3rd - red with a light-green center; drumsticks and shafts of halberds and spontoons - black.

Sevsk Regiment of the Livonia [Livland, Liflyandskaya] Inspectorate:

Turquoise collar and cuffs; yellow shoulder straps; grenadier caps with turquoise crowns and yellow bands; pompons on grenadier caps and hats: in the 1st battalion - white with a turquoise; in the 2nd - yellow with a turquoise center; in the 3rd - red with a turquoise center; drumsticks and shafts of halberds and spontoons - black (Illus. 1346).

Sofiya Regiment of the same Inspectorate:

Turquoise collar and cuffs; light-raspberry shoulder straps; grenadier caps with turquoise crowns and light-raspberry bands; pompons on grenadier caps and hats: in the 1st battalion - white with a grey center; in the 2nd - yellow with a grey center; in the 3rd - red with a grey center; drumsticks and shafts of halberds and spontoons - coffee colored.

Reval Regiment of the same Inspectorate:

Turquoise collar, cuffs, and shoulder straps; grenadier caps with turquoise crowns and bands; pompons on grenadier caps and hats: in the 1st battalion - white with a light-green center; in the 2nd - yellow with a light-green center; in the 3rd - red with a light-green center; drumsticks and shafts of halberds and spontoons - white.

Tobolsk Regiment of the same Inspectorate:

Turquoise collar and cuffs; rose shoulder straps; grenadier caps with turquoise crowns and rose bands; pompons on grenadier caps and hats: in the 1st battalion - white with a light-green center; in the 2nd - yellow with a light-green center; in the 3rd - red with a light-green center; drumsticks and shafts of halberds and spontoons - white.

Dnieper Regiment of the same Inspectorate:

Turquoise collar and cuffs; light-green shoulder straps; grenadier caps with turquoise crowns and light-green bands; pompons on grenadier caps and hats: in the 1st battalion - white with a rose center; in the 2nd - yellow with a rose center; in the 3rd - red with a rose center; drumsticks and shafts of halberds and spontoons - pale yellow.

Chernigov Regiment of the same Inspectorate:

Turquoise collar and cuffs; grey shoulder straps; grenadier caps with turquoise crowns and grey bands; pompons on grenadier caps and hats: in the 1st battalion - white with a yellow center; in the 2nd - yellow; in the 3rd - red with a yellow center, drumsticks and shafts of halberds and spontoons - black.

Tula Regiment of the Lithuania Inspectorate:

Light-green collar and cuffs; white shoulder straps; grenadier caps with light-green crowns and white bands; pompons on grenadier caps and hats: in the 1st battalion - white with a light-green center; in the 2nd - yellow with a light-green center; in the 3rd - red with a light-green center; drumsticks and shafts of halberds and spontoons - coffee colored (Illus. 1347).

Pskov Regiment of the same Inspectorate:

Light-green collar and cuffs; yellow shoulder straps; grenadier caps with light-green crowns and yellow bands; pompons on grenadier caps and hats: in the 1st battalion - white; in the 2nd - yellow with a white center; in the 3rd - red with a white center; drumsticks and shafts of halberds and spontoons - pale yellow.

Murom Regiment of the same Inspectorate:

Light-green collar and cuffs; light-raspberry shoulder straps; grenadier caps with light-green crowns and light-raspberry bands; pompons on grenadier caps and hats: in the 1st battalion - white with a light-green center; in the 2nd - yellow with a light-green center; in the 3rd - red with a light-green center; drumsticks and shafts of halberds and spontoons - coffee colored.

Rostov Regiment of the same Inspectorate:
Light-green collar and cuffs; turquoise shoulder straps; grenadier caps with light-green crowns and turquoise bands; pompons on grenadier caps and hats: in the 1st battalion - white with a yellow center; in the 2nd - yellow; in the 3rd - red with a yellow center; drumsticks and shafts of halberds and spontoons - coffee colored.

Nizovsk Regiment of the same Inspectorate:
Light-green collar and cuffs; rose shoulder straps; grenadier caps with light-green crowns and rose bands; pompons on grenadier caps and hats: in the 1st battalion - white with a rose center; in the 2nd - yellow with a rose center; in the 3rd - red with a rose center; drumsticks and shafts of halberds and spontoons - white.

Archangel Regiment of the same Inspectorate:
Light-green collar, cuffs, and shoulder straps; grenadier caps with light-green crowns and bands; pompons on grenadier caps and hats: in the 1st battalion - white with a turqoise center; in the 2nd - yellow with a turquoise center; in the 3rd - red with a turquoise center; drumsticks and shafts of halberds and spontoons - black.

Old-Ingermanland Regiment of the Brest Inspectorate:
Pale-yellow collar and cuffs; red shoulder straps; grenadier caps with pale-yellow crowns and red bands; pompons on grenadier caps and hats: in the 1st battalion - white with a yellow center; in the 2nd - yellow; in the 3rd - red with a yellow center; drumsticks and shafts of halberds and spontoons - white (Illus. 1348).

Ryazhsk Regiment of the same Inspectorate:
Pale-yellow collar and cuffs; white shoulder straps; grenadier caps with pale-yellow crowns and white bands; pompons on grenadier caps and hats: in the 1st battalion - white with a turquoise center; in the 2nd - yellow with a turquoise center; in the 3rd - red with a turquoise center; drumsticks and shafts of halberds and spontoons - black.

Viborg Regiment of the same Inspectorate:
Pale-yellow collar and cuffs; yellow shoulder straps; grenadier caps with pale-yellow crowns and yellow bands; pompons on grenadier caps and hats: in the 1st battalion - white; in the 2nd - yellow with a white center; in the 3rd - red with a white center; drumsticks and shafts of halberds and spontoons - coffee colored.

Apsheron Regiment of the same Inspectorate:
Pale-yellow collar and cuffs; light-raspberry shoulder straps; grenadier caps with pale-yellow crowns and light-raspberry bands; pompons on grenadier caps and hats: in the 1st battalion - white with a light-green center; in the 2nd - yellow with a light-green center; in the 3rd - red with a light-green center; drumsticks and shafts of halberds and spontoons - black.

Azov Regiment of the same Inspectorate:
Pale-yellow collar and cuffs; turquoise shoulder straps; grenadier caps with pale-yellow crowns and turqoise bands; pompons on grenadier caps and hats: in the 1st battalion - white with a red center; in the 2nd - yellow with a red center; in the 3rd - red; drumsticks and shafts of halberds and spontoons - pale yellow.

Smolensk Regiment of the Ukraine Inspectorate:
Rose collar and cuffs; yellow shoulder straps; grenadier caps with rose crowns and yellow bands; pompons on grenadier caps and hats: in the 1st battalion - white with a yellow center; in the 2nd - yellow; in the 3rd - red with a yellow center; drumsticks and shafts of halberds and spontoons - pale yellow (Illus. 1349).

Bryansk Regiment of the same Inspectorate:
Rose collar and cuffs; light-raspberry shoulder straps; grenadier caps with rose crowns and light-raspberry bands; pompons on grenadier caps and hats: in the 1st battalion - white with a light-green center; in the 2nd - yellow with a light-green center; in the 3rd - red with a light-green center; drumsticks and shafts of halberds and spontoons - coffee colored.

Ladoga Regiment of the Dniester Inspectorate:
Lilac [*lilovyi*] collar and cuffs; yellow shoulder straps; grenadier caps with lilac crowns and yellow bands; pompons on grenadier caps and hats: in the 1st battalion - white with a rose center; in the 2nd - yellow with a rose center; in the 3rd - red with a rose center; drumsticks and shafts of halberds and spontoons - black (Illus. 1350).

Vladimir Regiment of the same Inspectorate:
Lilac green collar and cuffs; light-raspberry shoulder straps; grenadier caps with lilac crowns and light-raspberry bands; pompons on grenadier caps and hats: in the 1st battalion - white with a light-green center; in the 2nd - yellow with a light-green center; in the 3rd - red with a light-green center; drumsticks and shafts of halberds and spontoons - white.

New-Ingermanland Regiment of the same Inspectorate:

Lilac collar and cuffs; turquoise shoulder straps; grenadier caps with light-green crowns and turquoise bands; pompons on grenadier caps and hats: in the 1st battalion - white with a lilac center; in the 2nd - yellow with a lilac center; in the 3rd - red with a lilac center; drumsticks and shafts of halberds and spontoons - coffee colored.

Aleksopol Regiment of the same Inspectorate:

Lilac collar and cuffs; rose shoulder straps; grenadier caps with lilac crowns and rose bands; pompons on grenadier caps and hats: in the 1st battalion - white with a light-green center; in the 2nd - yellow with a light-green center; in the 3rd - red with a light-green center; drumsticks and shafts of halberds and spontoons - black.

Kozlov Regiment of the same Inspectorate:

Lilac collar and cuffs; light-green shoulder straps; grenadier caps with lilac crowns and light-green bands; pompons on grenadier caps and hats: in the 1st battalion - white with a grey center; in the 2nd - yellow with a grey center; in the 3rd - red with a grey center; drumsticks and shafts of halberds and spontoons - white.

Yaroslavl Regiment of the same Inspectorate:

Lilac collar and cuffs; grey shoulder straps; grenadier caps with lilac crowns and grey bands; pompons on grenadier caps and hats: in the 1st battalion - white with a turquoise center; in the 2nd - yellow with a turquoise center; in the 3rd - red with a turquoise center; drumsticks and shafts of halberds and spontoons - pale yellow.

Nizhnii-Novgorod Regiment of the same Inspectorate:

Lilac collar, cuffs, and shoulder straps; grenadier caps with lilac crowns and bands; pompons on grenadier caps and hats: in the 1st battalion - white with a yellow center; in the 2nd - yellow; in the 3rd - red with a yellow center; drumsticks and shafts of halberds and spontoons - coffee colored.

Belev Regiment of the Crimea Inspectorate:

Blanched [*planshevyi*] collar and cuffs; red shoulder straps; grenadier caps with blanched crowns and red bands; pompons on grenadier caps and hats: in the 1st battalion - white with a yellow center; in the 2nd - yellow; in the 3rd - red with a yellow center; drumsticks and shafts of halberds and spontoons - coffee colored (Illus. 1350).

Sevastopol Regiment of the same Inspectorate:

Blanched collar and cuffs; white shoulder straps; grenadier caps with blanched crowns and white bands; pompons on grenadier caps and hats: in the 1st battalion - white with a light-green center; in the 2nd - yellow with a light-green center; in the 3rd - red with a light-green center; drumsticks and shafts of halberds and spontoons - black.

Troitsk Regiment of the same Inspectorate:

Blanched collar and cuffs; yellow shoulder straps; grenadier caps with blanched crowns and yellow bands; pompons on grenadier caps and hats: in the 1st battalion - white with a red center; in the 2nd - yellow with a red center; in the 3rd - red; drumsticks and shafts of halberds and spontoons - pale yellow.

Vitebsk Regiment of the same Inspectorate:

Blanched collar and cuffs; light-raspberry shoulder straps; grenadier caps with blanched crowns and light-raspberry bands; pompons on grenadier caps and hats: in the 1st battalion - white, in the 2nd - yellow with a white center; in the 3rd - red with a white center; drumsticks and shafts of halberds and spontoons - white.

Suzdal Regiment of the Caucasus Inspectorate:

Dark-blue [*sinii*] collar and cuffs; white shoulder straps; grenadier caps with dark-blue crowns and white bands; pompons on grenadier caps and hats: in the 1st battalion - white with a yellow center; in the 2nd - yellow, in the 3rd - red with a yellow center; drumsticks and shafts of halberds and spontoons - pale yellow.

Tiflis Regiment of the same Inspectorate:

Dark-blue collar and cuffs; yellow shoulder straps; grenadier caps with dark-blue crowns and yellow bands; pompons on grenadier caps and hats: in the 1st battalion - white with a light-green center; in the 2nd - yellow with a light-green center; in the 3rd - red with a light-green center; drumsticks and shafts of halberds and spontoons - black.

Kabarda Regiment of the same Inspectorate:

Dark-blue collar and cuffs; light-raspberry shoulder straps; grenadier caps with dark-blue crowns and light-raspberry bands; pompons on grenadier caps and hats: in the 1st battalion - white with a turquoise center; in the 2nd - yellow with a turquoise center; in the 3rd - red with a turquoise center; drumsticks and shafts of halberds and spontoons - white.

Kazan Regiment of the same Inspectorate:

Dark-blue collar and cuffs; turquoise shoulder straps; grenadier caps with dark-blue crowns and turquoise bands; pompons on grenadier caps and hats: in the 1st battalion - white; in the 2nd - yellow with a white center; in the 3rd - red with a white center; drumsticks and shafts of halberds and spontoons - pale yellow.

Polotsk Regiment of the Smolensk Inspectorate:
White collar and cuffs; yellow shoulder straps; grenadier caps with white crowns and yellow bands; pompons on grenadier caps and hats: in the 1st battalion - white with a light-green center; in the 2nd - yellow with a light-green center; in the 3rd - red with a light-green center; drumsticks and shafts of halberds and spontoons - black (Illus. 1351).

Perm Regiment of the same Inspectorate:
White collar and cuffs; light-raspberry shoulder straps; grenadier caps with white crowns and light-raspberry bands; pompons on grenadier caps and hats: in the 1st battalion - white with a yellow center; in the 2nd - yellow; in the 3rd - red with a yellow center; drumsticks and shafts of halberds and spontoons - white.

Uglich Regiment of the same Inspectorate:
White collar and cuffs; turquoise shoulder straps; grenadier caps with white crowns and turquoise bands; pompons on grenadier caps and hats: in the 1st battalion - white with a turquoise center; in the 2nd - yellow with a turquoise center; in the 3rd - red with a turquoise center; drumsticks and shafts of halberds and spontoons - pale yellow.

Kursk Regiment of the same Inspectorate:
White collar and cuffs; rose shoulder straps; grenadier caps with white crowns and rose bands; pompons on grenadier caps and hats: in the 1st battalion - white with a rose center; in the 2nd - yellow with a rose center; in the 3rd - red with a rose center; drumsticks and shafts of halberds and spontoons - black.

Voronezh Regiment of the same Inspectorate:
White collar and cuffs; light-green shoulder straps; grenadier caps with white crowns and light-green bands; pompons on grenadier caps and hats: in the 1st battalion - white with a light-green center; in the 2nd - yellow with a light-green center; in the 3rd - red with a light-green center; drumsticks and shafts of halberds and spontoons - white.

Moscow Regiment of the Kiev Inspectorate:
Light-raspberry collar and cuffs; red shoulder straps; grenadier caps with light-raspberry crowns and red bands; pompons on grenadier caps and hats: in the 1st battalion - white with a red center; in the 2nd - yellow with a red center; in the 3rd - red; drumsticks and shafts of halberds and spontoons - white (Illus. 1352).

Butyrsk Regiment of the same Inspectorate:
Light-raspberry collar and cuffs; white shoulder straps; grenadier caps with light-raspberry crowns and white bands; pompons on grenadier caps and hats: in the 1st battalion - white with a turquoise center; in the 2nd - yellow with a turquoise center; in the 3rd - red with a turquoise center; drumsticks and shafts of halberds and spontoons - black.

Kolyvan Regiment of the same Inspectorate:
Light-raspberry collar and cuffs; yellow shoulder straps; grenadier caps with light-raspberry crowns and yellow bands; pompons on grenadier caps and hats: in the 1st battalion - white with a rose center; in the 2nd - yellow with a rose center; in the 3rd - red with a rose center; drumsticks and shafts of halberds and spontoons - white.

Novgorod Regiment of the same Inspectorate:
Light-raspberry collar, cuffs, and shoulder straps; grenadier caps with light-raspberry crowns and bands; pompons on grenadier caps and hats: in the 1st battalion - white; in the 2nd - yellow with a white center; in the 3rd - red with a white center; drumsticks and shafts of halberds and spontoons - white.

Vyatka Regiment of the same Inspectorate:
Light-raspberry collar and cuffs; turquoise shoulder straps; grenadier caps with light-raspberry crowns and turquoise bands; pompons on grenadier caps and hats: in the 1st battalion - white with a yellow center; in the 2nd - yellow; in the 3rd - red with a yellow center; drumsticks and shafts of halberds and spontoons - coffee colored.

Narva Regiment of the same Inspectorate:
Light-raspberry collar and cuffs; rose shoulder straps; grenadier caps with light-raspberry crowns and rose bands; pompons on grenadier caps and hats: in the 1st battalion - white with a light-green center; in the 2nd - yellow with a light-green center; in the 3rd - red with a light-green center; drumsticks and shafts of halberds and spontoons - white.

Poltava Regiment of the same Inspectorate:
Light-raspberry collar and cuffs; light-green shoulder straps; grenadier caps with light-raspberry crowns and light-green bands; pompons on grenadier caps and hats: in the 1st battalion - white with a light-green center; in the 2nd - yellow with a light-green center; in the 3rd - red with a light-green center; drumsticks and shafts of halberds and spontoons - white.

Navaginsk Regiment of the Moscow Inspectorate:
Orange collar and cuffs; white shoulder straps; grenadier caps with orange crowns and white bands; pompons on grenadier caps and hats: in the 1st battalion - white with a light-green center; in the 2nd - yellow with a light-green center; in the 3rd - red with a light-green center; drumsticks and shafts of halberds and spontoons - pale yellow (Illus. 1353).

Tambov Regiment of the same Inspectorate:
Orange collar and cuffs; yellow shoulder straps; grenadier caps with orange crowns and yellow bands; pompons on grenadier caps and hats: in the 1st battalion - white with a light-green center; in the 2nd - yellow with a light-green center; in the 3rd - red with a light-green center; drumsticks and shafts of halberds and spontoons - black.

Ukraine Regiment of the same Inspectorate:
Orange collar and cuffs; light-raspberry shoulder straps; grenadier caps with orange crowns and light-raspberry bands; pompons on grenadier caps and hats: in the 1st battalion - white with a grey center; in the 2nd - yellow with a grey center; in the 3rd - red with a grey center; drumsticks and shafts of halberds and spontoons - white.

Schlüsselburg Regiment of the same Inspectorate:
Orange collar and cuffs; turquoise shoulder straps; grenadier caps with orange crowns and turquoise bands; pompons on grenadier caps and hats: in the 1st battalion - white; in the 2nd - yellow with a white center; in the 3rd - red with a white center; drumsticks and shafts of halberds and spontoons - black.

Nasheburg Regiment of the same Inspectorate:
Orange collar and cuffs; rose shoulder straps; grenadier caps with orange crowns and rose bands; pompons on grenadier caps and hats: in the 1st battalion - white with a yellow center; in the 2nd - yellow; in the 3rd - red with a yellow center; drumsticks and shafts of halberds and spontoons - coffee colored.

Orel Regiment of the same Inspectorate:
Orange collar and cuffs; light-green shoulder straps; grenadier caps with orange crowns and light-green bands; pompons on grenadier caps and hats: in the 1st battalion - white with a turquoise center; in the 2nd - yellow with a turquoise center; in the 3rd - red with a turquoise center; drumsticks and shafts of halberds and spontoons - pale yellow.

Saratov Regiment of the same Inspectorate:
Orange collar and cuffs; grey shoulder straps; grenadier caps with orange crowns and grey bands; pompons on grenadier caps and hats: in the 1st battalion - white with a lilac center; in the 2nd - yellow with a lilac center; in the 3rd - red with a lilac center; drumsticks and shafts of halberds and spontoons - white.

Staryi-Oskol Regiment of the same Inspectorate:
 Orange collar and cuffs; lilac shoulder straps; grenadier caps with orange crowns and lilac bands; pompons on grenadier caps and hats: in the 1st battalion - white with a rose center; in the 2nd - yellow with a rose center; in the 3rd - red with a rose center; drumsticks and shafts of halberds and spontoons - white.

Olonets Regiment of the same Inspectorate:
Orange collar and cuffs; dark-blue shoulder straps; grenadier caps with orange crowns and dark-blue bands; pompons on grenadier caps and hats: in the 1st battalion - white with a dark-blue center; in the 2nd - yellow with a dark-blue center; in the 3rd - red with a dark-blue center; drumsticks and shafts of halberds and spontoons - white.

Rylsk Regiment of the Orenburg Inspectorate:
Camel-colored [*verblyuzhii*] collar and cuffs; red shoulder straps; grenadier caps with camel-colored crowns and red bands; pompons on grenadier caps and hats: in the 1st battalion - white with a red center; in the 2nd - yellow with a red center; in the 3rd - red; drumsticks and shafts of halberds and spontoons - coffee colored (Illus. 1354).

Ufa Regiment of the same Inspectorate:
Camel-colored collar and cuffs; white shoulder straps; grenadier caps with camel-colored crowns and white bands; pompons on grenadier caps and hats: in the 1st battalion - white; in the 2nd - yellow with a white center; in the 3rd - red with a white center; drumsticks and shafts of halberds and spontoons - black.

Yekaterinburg Regiment of the same Inspectorate:
Camel-colored collar and cuffs; yellow shoulder straps; grenadier caps with camel-colored crowns and yellos bands; pompons on grenadier caps and hats: in the 1st battalion - white with a yellow center; in the 2nd - yellow; in the 3rd - red with a yellow center; drumsticks and shafts of halberds and spontoons - coffee colored.

Shirvan Regiment of the Siberia Inspectorate:
Grey collar and cuffs; red shoulder straps; grenadier caps with grey crowns and red bands; pompons on grenadier caps and hats: in the 1st battalion - white with a red center; in the 2nd - yellow with a red center; in the 3rd - red; drumsticks and shafts of halberds and spontoons - white (Illus. 1355).

Tomsk Regiment of the same Inspectorate:
Grey collar and cuffs; white shoulder straps; grenadier caps with grey crowns and white bands; pompons on grenadier caps and hats: in the 1st battalion - white; in the 2nd - yellow with a white center; in the 3rd - red with a white center; drumsticks and shafts of halberds and spontoons - coffee colored.

Seleginsk Regiment of the same Inspectorate:
Grey collar and cuffs; yellow shoulder straps; grenadier caps with grey crowns and yellow bands; pompons on grenadier caps and hats: in the 1st battalion - white with a yellow center; in the 2nd - yellow; in the 3rd - red with a yellow center; drumsticks and shafts of halberds and spontoons - black (752).

27 October 1802— Generals and field and company-grade officers of Musketeer regiments are permitted to wear **riding trousers** [*reituzy*] when on campaign, the same as described above for Grenadier regiments (753).

16 May 1803— For the **Musketeer regiments** authorized on this day: *in the St.-Petersburg Inspectorate* — the **Petrovsk**, *in the Liflyand* — the **Kopore**, *in the Lithuania* — the **Volhynia**, *in the Brest* — the **Podolsk**, *in the Ukraine* — the **Galich**, *in the Dniester* — the **Crimea**, and *in the Caucasus* — the **Vologda**, colors on the coats are prescribed in accordance with the Inspectorates to which they are assigned (754).

29 June 1803— Generals, field-grade officers, and adjutants of Musketeer regiments are given new-pattern **shabracks** and **holsters**, the same as authorized at this same time for Grenadier regiments (755).

19 August 1803— All lower ranks in Musketeer regiments who are authorized hats are given **shakos** [*shapki*] of the same pattern as received at this time by noncombatants in Grenadier regiments (Illus. 1356) (756).

19 October 1803— All noncommissioned officers of Musketeer regiments are to have two **shoulder straps** on their coats and greatcoats instead of one (757).

3 August 1804— The **Saratov Musketeer Regiment** is assigned lilac shoulder straps; the **Sevastopol Regiment**, instead of light raspberry - rose; the **Vologda Regiment**, instead of rose - light green (758).

15 November 1804— Musketeer regiments of the **Dniester Inspectorate** are ordered to have: dark-green collars and cuff flaps, with red piping; red cuffs; dark-green grenadier caps; the back of these caps are to be the same color as the shoulder straps, and the shoulder straps are to be according to the regiment:

    Nizhegorod . . . . - red.
    Vladimir . . . . - white.
    Yaroslav . . . .- yellow.
    Aleksopol . . . .- raspberry.
    Kozlov . . . .- turquoise.
    New-Ingermanland . . . .- rose.
[Here Zvegintsov adds the Ladoga Regiment with light green — M.C.]
    Crimea . . . . - grey (759).

In the same year of 1804, generals and field and company-grade officers of Musketeer regiments were given **hats** with buttonhole loops of narrow gold galloon and high plumes, according to the pattern prescribed at this time for Grenadier generals and officers (760).

19 January 1805— For Musketeer regiments of the **Caucasus Inspectorate**, for greater distinction between personnel of different regiments when they are in **forage caps**, it is permitted to sew cloth tape in the regimental color onto the upper edge of the cap band, i.e. of that color prescribed for shoulder straps, 7/8 inch wide and leaving a bit of the band above as edging (761).

26 January 1805— Of the number of noncommissioned officers in the second and third battalions of Musketeer regiments, all of whom are prescribed halberds according to the table of 30 April 1802, four men of each company are ordered to have muskets and cartridge pouches, following the example of the companies in Grenadier regiments (762).

13 February 1805— The cloth **shakos** used in Musketeer regiments since 1803 are replaced by new ones of the same pattern as prescribed at this time for Grenadier regiments, but without the small grenade and without the plume, instead of which Musketeers keep the pompons they already have (Illus. 1357). Grenadiers are given the same shakos but with a grenade and plume (763).

23 December 1805— The directive concerning the field uniform of generals and field and company-grade officers of Grenadier regiments in the **Caucasus Inspectorate** are also extended with equal force to these ranks in its Musketeer regiments (764).

5 January 1806— The newly formed **Musketeer regiments** are assigned shoulder straps as follows: *Kaluga* - lilac, *Mogilev* - grey, *Kostroma* - lilac, *Vilna* - light green, *Penza* - grey, *Estonia [Estland]* - turquoise, and *Odessa* - grey (765). The following orders, mentioned above for Grenadier regiments, were extended with equal force to Musketeer regiments: **1 July 1806** — about the new uniform for doctors, and **1 October** of the same year — about the abolition of warm coats for lower ranks (766).

30 November 1806— The coats of newly formed Musketeer regiments are ordered to have:

Libau- sky-blue collar; red cuffs, flaps (with 5 buttons), and shoulder straps.

Kamchatka- red collar, cuffs, flaps (with 5 buttons), and shoulder straps.

[For the Kamchatka Regiment, Zvegintsov gives white collar, cuffs, and flaps, and red straps — M.C.]

Mingrelia- yellow collar and cuffs; red flaps (with 5 buttons) and shoulder straps.

Villmanstrand- red collar, cuffs, and flaps (with 5 buttons); shoulder straps white with red piping.

Brest- white collar; red cuffs and flaps (with 5 buttons); yellow shoulder straps.

Kremenchug- yellow collar; red cuffs and flaps (with 5 buttons); yellow shoulder straps.

Minsk- sky-blue collar; red cuffs and flaps (with 5 buttons); white shoulder straps.

Nyslott- green collar; red cuffs and flaps (with 5 buttons); white shoulder straps.

Okhotsk- sky-blue collar and cuffs; red flaps (with 5 buttons); yellow shoulder straps.

Pernau- white collar; red cuffs; white flaps (with 5 buttons); sky-blue shoulder straps (767).

The following orders, mentioned above for Grenadier regiments, were extended with equal force to Musketeer regiments: **2 December 1806** — about cutting lower ranks' queues; **10 March 1807** — about the abolition of spontoons and canes for officers; **17 September 1807** — about their wearing epaulettes; **7 November 1807** — about all regiments having red collars and cuffs; **15 December 1807** — about sewing divisional numbers onto shoulder straps and epaulettes; **19 December 1807** — about wearing swordbelts over the shoulder, changes to the swordknots, the removal of the seventh button on the coat's lower front, etc.; **23 December 1807** — about the introduction of winter pants with integral leggings [*kragi*] and summer ones with integral spats [*kozyrki*]; **28 January 1808** — about generals being authorized a parade dress coat and dark-green pants for daily use; **14 July 1808** — about the introduction of a new pattern of rectangular knapsacks, the rolling of greatcoats, and grenadier shakos having grenades with three flames and others having them with one flame, along with which the upper pompons in use since 1802 were discontinued; **2 November 1808** — about only combatants keeping the winter pants with leggings and the summer ones with spats; **5 November 1808** — about officers wearing knapsacks while on campaign; **12 November 1808** — about their being allowed to wear dark-green pants when not on duty; **November 1808** — about the new pattern of officers' gorgets being confirmed; **5 December 1808** — the same for halberd shafts and drumsticks; **11 February 1809** — about noncombatant lower ranks' forage caps being changed; **4 April 1809** — about noncommissioned officers having galloon not on the lower edge of the collar but on the upper; **8 April 1809** — about changes in the carrying of the greatcoat and knapsack (Illus. 1358); **30 May 1809** — about the replacement of noncommissioned officers' front pouches [*podsumki*] with ones [*sumy*] with crossbelts; **11 June 1809** — about cords for the shakos; **8 July 1809** — about the new pattern of generals' hats; **29 August 1809** — about only sergeants retaining halberds; **23 November 1809** — about colors for shako pompons; and **6 December 1809** — about officers being prescribed shakos. All these were applied to Musketeer regiments except for the last one about shakos, which in Musketeer regiments had plumes only for Grenadiers, while others had no plumes (768).

9 Januray 1810— **Shoulder straps** in Musketeer regiments are ordered to be:

1st Division: *Kexholm* - yellow.

2nd Division: *Polotsk* - dark green with red piping; *Yelets* - yellow; *Lithuania* - sky blue.

3rd Division: *Chernigov* - white; *Murom* - yellow; *Kopore* - dark green with red piping.

4th Division: *Tobolsk* - red; *Vilna* - yellow; *Volhynia* - white; *Kremenchug* - dark green with red piping; *Minsk* -sky blue.

5th Division: *Perm* - red; *Sevsk* - white; *Mogilev* - yellow; *Kaluga* - dark green with red piping.

6th Division: *Azov* - red; *Nizovsk* - yellow; *Reval* - dark green with red piping; *Uglich* - white; *Sofiya* - sky blue.

7th Division: *Pskov* - white; *Moscow* - yellow: *Vladimir* - dark green with red piping; *Podolia* - sky blue.

8th Division: *Archangel* - white; *Schlüsselburg*- yellow: *Voronezh* - dark green with red piping; *Old-Ingermanland* - sky blue.

9th Division: *Ryazhsk* - white; *Ukraine* - yellow; *Galich* - dark green with red piping; *Bialystok* - sky blue.

10th Division: *Yaroslav* - white; *Bryansk* - yellow; *Kursk* - dark green with red piping; *Crimea* - sky blue.

11th Division: *Nasheburg* - yellow; *Apsheron* - dark green with red piping; *Odessa* - sky blue.

12th Division: *Smolensk* - white; *Narva* - yellow; *Orel* - dark green with red piping; *New-Ingermanland* - sky blue.

13th Division: *Nizhnii-Novgorod* - red; *Ladoga* - white; *Aleksopol* - yellow; *Butyrsk* - dark green with red piping; *Poltava* - sky blue; *Estonia* - blanched.

14th Division: *Graf Arakcheev's Regiment* - red; *Tula* - white; *Tenginsk* - yellow; *Navaginsk* - dark green with red piping.

15th Divison: *Vitebsk* - red; *Kozlov* - white; *Kolyvan* - yellow; *Kura* - dark green with red piping.

16th Division: *Novgorod* - red; *Nyslott* - white; *Okhotsk* - yellow; *Kamchatka* - dark green with red piping; *Mingrelia* - sky blue.

17th Division: *Brest* - yellow; *Ryazan* - red; *Belozersk* - white; *Villmanstrand* - dark green with red piping.

18th Division: *Tambov* - red; *Dnieper* - white; *Kostroma* - yellow; *Yakutsk* - dark green with red piping.

19th Division: *Kazan* - red; *Suzdal* - white; *Belev* - yellow; *Sevastopol* - dark green with red piping; *Vologda* - sky blue.

20th Division: *Troitsk* - yellow; *Tiflis* - dark green with red piping; *Kabarda* - sky blue; *Saratov* - blanched.

21st Division: *Velikie-Luki* - red; *Neva* - white; *Petrovsk* - yellow; *Libau* - dark green with red piping; *Pernau* - sky blue.

22nd Division: *Viborg* - red; *Vyatka* - white; *Staryi-Oskol* - yellow; *Olonets*- dark green with red piping; *Penza* - sky blue.

23rd Division: *Rylsk* - white; *Yekaterinburg* - yellow.   24th Division, *Selenginsk* - red.

25th Division: *Shirvan* - red; *Ufa* - white; *Tomsk* - yellow (769).

The following directives, mentioned above for Grenadier regiments, extended with equal force to Musketeer regiments: **24 September 1810** — about having knapsack straps stitched and with bends at the shoulders; **17 January 1811** — about changes in the colors of shako cords; **29 January 1811** — about having officers' frock coats with red cuffs; **4 February 1811** — about the change in shako plumes; **22 February 1811** — about colors for pompons and swordknots; **23 September 1811** — about changing lower ranks' forage caps; **9 October 1811** — about the complete abolishment of halberds; and **3 November 1811** — about noncommissioned officers not having gloves. All these apply with equal force to Musketeer regiments, except that since 22 February 1811 plumes were authorized for Grenadiers alone, excluding Marksmen (770).

7 November 1811 — **Shoulder straps** are assigned for the newly established Infantry regiments of the **27th Division**: *Odessa* - red; *Vilna* - white; *Tarnopol* - yellow; *Simbirsk* - dark green (Illus. 1359) (771).

The following directives, mentioned above for Grenadier regiments, extended with equal force to Infantry regiments: **17 December 1811** — about the new uniform for noncombatant ranks; **1 January 1812** — concerning the introduction of a new-pattern shakos [*kivera*], the changes in the style of collars, leggings, and officers' boots (Illus. 1360), and officers having white appointments and brass, forged epaulettes; and **10 February 1812** — about noncombatant lower ranks wearing shoulder straps identical to those prescribed for combatants (772).

12 April 1812 — Musketeer regiments are assigned **shoulder straps** of the following colors:

3rd Division: *Chernigov* - red; *Murom* - white; *Reval* - yellow; *Kopore* - dark green with red piping.

4th Division: *Tobolsk* - red; *Volhynia* - white; *Kremenchug* - yellow; *Minsk* - dark green with red piping.

5th Division: *Perm* - red; *Sevsk* - white; *Mogilev* - yellow; *Kaluga* - dark green with red piping.

6th Division: *Azov* - red; *Uglich* - white; *Nizovsk* - yellow; *Bryansk* - dark green with red piping.

7th Division: *Pskov* - red; *Moscow* - white; *Libau* - yellow; *Sofiya* - dark green with red piping.

8th Division: *Archangel* - red; *Schlüsselburg* - white; *Old-Ingermanland* - yellow; *Ukraine* - dark green with red piping.

9th Division: *Nasheburg* - red; *Apsheron* - white; *Ryazhsk* - yellow; *Yakutsk* - dark green with red piping.

10th Division: *Yaroslavl*- red; *Kursk* - white; *Crimea* - yellow; *Bialystok* - dark green with red piping.

11th Division: *Kexholm* - red; *Yelets* - white; *Polotsk* - yellow; *Pernau* - dark green with red piping.

12th Division: *Smolensk* - red; *Narva* - white; *Aleksopol* - yellow; *New-Ingermanland* - dark green with red piping.

13th Division: *Velikie-Luki* - red; *Saratov* - white; *Galich* - yellow; *Penza* - dark green with red piping.

14th Division: *Tula* - red; *Tenginsk* - white; *Navaginsk* - yellow; *Estonia* - dark green with red piping.

15th Division: *Vitebsk* - red; *Kozlov* - white; *Kolyvan* - yellow; *Kura* - dark green with red piping.

16th Division: *Nyslott* - red; *Okhotsk* - white; *Kamchatka* - yellow; *Mingrelia* - dark green with red piping.

17th Division: *Ryazan* - red; *Belozersk* - white; *Brest* - yellow; *Villmanstrand* - dark green with red piping.

18th Division: *Vladimir* - red; *Tambovsk* - white; *Dnieper* - yellow; *Kostroma* - dark green with red piping.

19th Division: *Kazan* - red; *Suzdal* - white; *Belev* - yellow; *Sevastopol* - dark green with red piping; *Vologda* - sky blue.

20th Division: *Troitsk* - red; *Tiflis* - white; *Kabarda* - yellow.

21st Division: *Neva* - red; *Petrovsk* - white; *Lithuania* - yellow; *Podolia* - dark green with red piping.

22nd Division: *Viborg* - red; *Vyatka* - white; *Staryi-Oskol* - yellow; *Olonets* - dark green with red piping.

23nd Division: *Rylsk* - red; *Yekaterinburg* - white; *Selenginsk* - yellow.

24th Division: *Shirvan* - red; *Butyrsk* - white; *Ufa* - yellow; *Tomsk* - dark green with red piping.

25th Division: *Voronezh* - red.

26th Division: *Nizhegorod* - red; *Ladoga* - white; *Poltava* - yellow; *Orel* - dark green with red piping.

27th Division: *Odessa* - red; *Vilna* - white; *Tarnopol* - yellow; *Simbirsk* - dark green with red piping (773).

22 August 1814— The color yellow is discontinued for **shoulder straps**, and to replace it all the third regiments of Infantry divisions are to have blue [*svetlosinie*] shoulder straps (774).

The following directives mentioned above for Grenadier regiments were also applicable to Infantry regiments: **1814 and 1815** — concerning changes in the pattern for officers' riding trousers and the cockade on officers' hats; about the uniforms for drum majors, musicians, fifers, and drummers; about the pattern of the shako badge for distinction, etc. (775); **24 January 1816** — about having black scabbards for rapiers and swords; **13 April 1816** — about officers' uniforms for wear in the capitals and outside them; **7 May 1816** — about drum majors wearing coats with silver galloon; **13 May 1816** — about the introduction of covers for shakos, plumes, coats, etc.; **8 August 1817** — about the size of forage caps; **26 September 1817** — about rules for making and wearing shakos and other soldiers' accouterments. Only in the last point was there a difference from Grenadier regiments in that in Infantry regiments Grenadiers had shakos with a triple-flamed grenade and not with a plate as previously; and for Musketeers the grenade had only one flame and the shakos did not have scales, these being replaced by a black, stitched, leather strap sewn onto the right side where the two shako side straps came together and fastened with a brass coat button fixed onto the same place, but on the other side (Illus. 1360). Grenades on the pouches in Infantry regiments were the same as on the shakos, i.e. in Grenadier companies with three flames, and in Musketeer companies with one, and there was also the difference that drummers' crossbelts in Musketeer companies did not have three grenades, but only one (776).

8 December 1817— Musketeer regiments are given **leggings with spats** (777). In this same year it was ordered that Infantry regiments of the **Separate Lithuania Corps** be uniformed in the style of the 1st and 2nd Grenadiers, described above, except with the existing distinctions of Infantry regiments as opposed to Grenadier regiments (Illus. 1361) (778).

25 August 1818— Lower ranks of Infantry regiments are ordered to have **shoulder straps** on their coats and greatcoats: as long as the shoulder, 2 1/4 inches wide, with the number of division as before, 1 3/4 inches high, cut out 7/8 inch from the lower edge of the shoulder strap and backed with cloth stitched along the edges of the cutout: in the first regiments of a division, on their red shoulder straps - in yellow; in the second regiments, on their white shoulder straps - in red; in the third regiments, on their blue shoulder straps - in yellow; and in the fourth regiments, on green shoulder straps - in yellow. The flaps or **wings** over the shoulders of musicians' and drummers' coats are prescribed to be the same color as the shoulder straps, while the lace for the sewn-on stripes are completely white, 7/8 inch wide (779).

The following directives mentioned above for Grenadier regiments were also applied in equal measure to Infantry regiments: **25 January 1819** — about the colors of drumsticks and of the handles of entrenching tools; **4 April 1819** — about leggings not having spats; **10 April 1819** — about uniforms for signalers and the pattern for signal horns; **20 September 1820** — about changing officers' gorgets; **26 September 1823** — about all musicians having noncommissioned officers' distinctions; **16 January 1824** — about changes in shako cords, knapsack straps, and musket slings; and **29 March 1825** — about instituting stripes to be sewn onto the left sleeve in recognition of irreproachable service. To this must also be added that in 1825 Infantry regiments of the **Separate Lithuania Corps** received round, woolen ***pompons*** [*pompony*] for their shakos, colored according to the battalions and companies: for Marksmen [*strelki*] of the first Grenadier companies - yellow; of the second Grenadier companies - top half yellow, lower half green; of the third Grenadier companies - top half yellow, lower half blue [*svetlosinyaya*]; for Musketeers of the first battalions - white; of the second battalions - top half white, lower half green; of the third battalions - top half white, lower half blue (Illus. 1362). Officers were given the same pompons except in silver (780).

III. MARINE REGIMENTS.

16 March 1813— When **Marine regiments** were reassigned to the Department of the Army [*Voenno-sukhoputnoe vedomstvo*, literally "Department of Military Land Forces"], they had exactly the same uniform and armament, as well as organization, as Musketeer regiments, with the only difference being that their their collars, cuffs, turnbacks on the tails, and coat lining, instead of being red, and their pants, instead of being white, were all dark green with white piping, this piping also being on the cuff flaps (Illus. 1363). Shoulder straps in the 1st Marine Regiment were red with the number 25; in the 2nd - white with the same number; in the 3rd - yellow with the same number; in the 4th - dark green with red piping and the number 28, i.e. in accordance with the numbers of the divisions to which the regiments were assigned. Forage caps were the same as in Grenadier and Infantry regiments but with dark-green bands (Illus. 1364), and officers' shabracks were also like shabracks in these regiments except they were completely dark green with white piping along the edges (Illus. 1365) (781). Subsequently, all the changes concerning Infantry regiments which were already mentioned above were extended with equal force to Marine regiments (Illus. 1366) (782).

The **Caspian Marine Battalion**, consisting of four Musketeer companies, was uniformed and armed the same as Marine regiments, with red shoulder straps without any number (783).

IV. JÄGER REGIMENTS.

9 April 1801— Lower ranks are ordered to cut off their curls and have **queues** 7 inches long, tying them at the middle of the collar (784).

18 May 1801— Instead of white cloth **pants**, Jäger regiments are to be issued with dark-green linen ones, these being white for summer, reaching below the calf to the instep (785).

21 June 1801— The directive concerning generals and field and company-grade officers of the **St.-Petersburg garrison** wearing hats of a new pattern, and the directives of **15 January** and **17 March 1802** regulating the pattern and sewing of coats, are extended with equal force to Jäger regiments (786).

30 April 1802— Confirmation is given to a new **table of uniforms**, accouterments, and weapons for Jäger regiments, based on which, along with the two preceeding directives, *Jäger privates* are prescribed: *coat* [*mundir*] or *caftan* [*kaftan*]; *pants* [*pantalony*]; *boots*; *neckcloth*; *forage cap*; *hat* [*shlyapa*]; *greatcoat*; *warm coat* [*fufaika*]; *musket with bayonet*, or *rifle* [*shtutser*] with *sword-bayonet* [*kortik*]; *swordbelt*; *ammunition pouch* [*patrontash*]; *knapsack* and *water flask*.

The *coat* was prescribed to be of the same pattern as was authorized at this time for Grenadier and Musketeer regiments except it was light green with similar lining and turnbacks on the tails, without shoulder straps; with a collar and cuffs in a special color for each regiment and with piping along the cuff flaps and tail turnbacks of the same color as the collar (Illus. 1367).

Pants, also of the same pattern as for grenadiers and musketeers but light green with piping of the same color as the collar (Illus. 1367), but of white linen in summer.

Boots, neckcloth, and forage cap- the same as in Grenadier and Musketeer regiments but the last being light green with the band and trim in the same color as the collar (Illus. 1367) or without any band at all.

Hat, height: 7 1/2 inches in front, 7 7/8 inches in back, with 4 3/8 inches between the crown and ends, tied with a black cord and not having any other decoration except for a flat, brass button and three small woolen tassels [i.e. the two tassels in the corners and the main pompon — M.C.] colored according to the special list below (Illus. 1368).

Greatcoat, grey, with a collar of the same color as on the coat, differing from grenadier and musketeer greatcoats only in that it had no shoulder straps (Illus. 1368).

The *warm coat* was the same as in grenadier and musketeer regiments.

Musket with flat bayonet, but for twelve men in each company— *rifle with sword-bayonet*. These had slings and lock covers [*ognivnye chekhly*] of red Russian leather (Illus. 1369).

Swordbelt, with a small frog sewn to it for the scabbard (either for the bayonet or the sword-bayonet), and with a brass buckle for fastening on the left side of the body; made from black, polished leather, just like the scabbard (Illus. 1369).

Ammunition pouch, of black leather, long enough to wrap around the front of the Jäger, from the right side to the back (Illus. 1369).

Knapsack and water flask, of the same issue as in Grenadier and Musketeer regiments but with black straps, and worn by Jägers not over the right shoulder, but over the left.

Noncommissioned officers had gold galloon on the collar and cuffs; tassels on the hat were white with a mixture of black and orange; canes [*trosti*] were worn on the left side. They were authorized rifles, sword-bayonets, and all other armaments, as well as all accouterments, identical to those prescribed for private Jägers (Illus. 1370).

Company drummers had tape sewn onto the coat and drums, the same as in Grenadier and Musketeer regiments, but drumsticks were black. Instead of sword-bayonets they were prescribed swords [*tesaki*] identical to those for Grenadier and Musketeer drummers, with company swordknots (Illus. 1371).

Battalion and *regimental drummers* and *hornists* [more exactly *waldhornists* [*voltornisty*] - M.C.] - all of noncommissioned-officer rank - were distinguished from company drummers in exactly the same way as in Grenadier and Musketeer regiments (Illus. 1372 and 1373).

Company-grade officers had uniforms as well as rapiers [*shpagi*], swordknots, swordbelts, sashes, and canes that were identical to those used at this time by Grenadier and Musketeer officers, except that the coats were light green with a collar, cuffs, and piping that were of the special regimental color. Their pants were also light green, with piping the same color as the collar; green plumes, but they were not authorized gorgets or spontoons (Illus. 1374).

Field-grade officers were distinguished from company-grade officers only in having boots with spurs (Illus. 1376).

Generals were similar to field-grade officers but they had additional white plumage on the hat [around the sides — M.C.] (Illus. 1376).

Noncombatant ranks - holding the same titles as in the previous regiments—were also uniformed the same, except the caftans had no shoulder straps (787).

6 June 1802— Confirmation is given to a listing of *pompon colors* on Jäger hats, which along with the above-mentioned directive of 17 March and table of 30 April is the basis of the following distinctions between the existing nineteen Jäger regiments:

1st Regiment— pale-yellow collar, cuffs, and piping (Illus. 1367); the center of the hat pompon is dark green while the surrounding part is (as in all the other regiments): for the 1st battalion - white; for the 2nd - yellow; and for the 3rd - red. *2nd Regiment*- collar, cuffs, piping, and center of the pompon - rose (Illus. 1367). *3rd Regiment*- collar, cuffs, piping, and center of the pompon - red (Illus. 1368). *4th Regiment*- collar, cuffs, piping, and center of the pompon - grey (Illus. 1368). *5th Regiment*- collar, cuffs, piping, and center of the pompon -turquoise (Illus. 1369). *6th Regiment*- collar, cuffs, and piping - fire colored [*ognevye*]; center of the pompon - light green (Illus. 1369). *7th Regiment*- collar, cuffs, piping, and center of the pompon - white (Illus. 1369). *8th Regiment*- collar, cuffs, piping, and center of the pompon - dark blue [*sinie*] (Illus. 1370). *9th Regiment*- collar, cuffs, piping, and center of the pompon - yellow (Illus. 1370). *10th Regiment*- collar, cuffs, piping, and center of the pompon - black (Illus. 1371). *11th Regiment*- collar, cuffs, and piping - apricot; center of the pompon - light green (Illus. 1372). *12th Regiment*- collar, cuffs, and piping - light raspberry; center of the pompon - light green (Illus. 1372). *13th Regiment*- collar, cuffs, and piping - blanched; center of the pompon - light green (Illus. 1373). *14th Regiment*- collar, cuffs, piping, and center of the pompon - chestnut colored [*kashtanovye*] (Illus. 1373). *15th Regiment*- collar, cuffs, piping, and center of the pompon - light iron colored [*svetlozheleznye*] (Illus. 1374). *16th Regiment*- collar, cuffs, piping, and center of the pompon - camel colored (Illus. 1374). *17th Regiment*- collar, cuffs, piping, and center of the pompon - violet [*fioletovye*] (Illus. 1375). *18th Regiment*- collar, cuffs, piping, and center of the pompon - brown (Illus. 1376). *19th Regiment*- collar, cuffs, piping, and center of the pompon - lilac (Illus. 1376)(788).

16 September 1802—Combatant lower ranks of Jäger regiments, in place of their previous tricorn **hats**, were given round ones of the same size as those established in 1803 for Musketeer regiments and with the same cockades and pompons [*kokardy i kistochki*] as on these (Illus. 1377). Noncommissioned officers, in addition, also had gold galloon around the upper edge (789).

22 June 1803—The collar, cuffs, and piping on the pants for the newly formed **20th Jäger Regiment** are prescribed to be dark green (Illus. 1378) (790).

5 January 1804—**Drummers' crossbelts** and **hoops** in Jäger regiments are ordered to be black.

12 April 1804—Generals and field and company-grade officers of Jäger regiments are given **shabracks** and **holsters** of the patterns confirmed for Grenadier and Musketeer regiments on 29 June 1803, but in light green with trim (between the strips of galloon) and piping (around) of the same color as the collar, the same being also ordered for the band as well as trim, ring, and tassel on forage caps (792).

4 August 1804—In Jäger regiments **musket and rifle slings** are ordered to be black instead of red. In this same year generals and field and company-grade officers of these regiments were given **hats** with a buttonhole loop of narrow, gold galloon, with the high, green plumes as before (793).

8 September 1805—The collars and cuffs of the newly established *21st* and *22nd Jäger Regiments* are ordered to be: for the first—red with white piping; for the second—white with red piping. For both, the piping on the pants is to be the same color as the collar (Illus. 1379) (794).

23 December 1805—The permission given to generals and officers of Grenadier and Musketeer regiments of the **Caucasus Inspectorate** to wear the same headdress as the soldiers is extended with equal force to the Jäger regiments of this Inspectorate (795).

27 January 1806—The newly formed **23rd Jäger Regiment** is prescribed orange collars and cuffs with white piping, while pants piping is orange (Illus. 1380).

20 June 1806—Newly formed **Jäger regiments** are prescribed collars and cuffs as follows: for the **24th**—light green, the same color as the coat, with sky-blue piping; for the **25th**—pale yellow, with red piping; for the **26th**—dark blue, with red piping. Pants piping for all three is to be the same color as the collar (Illus. 1381) (797).

1 July 1806—The new-pattern uniforms described above for **doctors** in Grenadier regiments are likewise for Jäger regiments (798).

18 October 1806—The ammunition pouches [*patrontashi*] used by Jäger regiments are replaced by **front pouches** [*podsumki*], 13 1/8 inches long and 5 inches wide (799).

2 December 1806—Lower ranks are ordered to cut their **hair** very short; but generals and field and company-grade officers are in this case allowed to proceed according to their own wishes (800).

31 December 1806—The newly formed **27th, 28th, 29th, 30th, 31st, and 32nd Jäger regiments** are designated to have light-green collars; the lining to the collar, piping along the edges of the collar and turnbacks of the tails, for officers also along the edges of the pocket flaps, as well as on the cuffs, and piping along the side seams of the pants, are all as follows: 27th Regiment —red (Illus. 1382); 28th —yellow (Illus. 1383); 29th —turquoise (Illus. 1383); 30th—white (Illus. 1385); 31st —raspberry (Illus. 1385); 32nd —black (Illus. 1385) (801).

17 September 1807—Generals and field and company-grade officers of Jäger regiments are given **epaulettes** of the same pattern as those received by these same ranks in Grenadier and Musketeer regiments (802).

26 September 1807—Instead of front pouches [*podsumki*], all Jäger regiments are ordered to have *pouches* [*sumy*] of the same pattern as used in Grenadier and Musketeer regiments, but without badges and on black crossbelts. At this same time, the round hats in use are replaced by *shakos* [*shapki*] of the same pattern as those confirmed for Musketeer regiments in 1803 (Illus. 1386) (803).

7 November 1807—For all Jäger regiments the light-green color of the **coat** is changed to **dark green**, and consequently officers' shabracks are also ordered to be completely dark green, edged around with red piping (Illus. 1387) (804).

19 December 1807—Lower ranks of Jäger regiments are ordered to wear **swordbelts** over the left shoulder, these being in all ways the same as those introduced at this time for Grenadier and Musketeer regiments, except with the white color changed to black. *Shakos* [*kivera*] are also introduced for Jägers, trimmed with black leather (Illus. 1388) (805). [Note by M.C. - Almost certainly, Viskovatov should have written "over the right shoulder" in regard to swordbelts.]

23 December 1807—Lower ranks of Jäger regiments are given summer and winter **pants** and **boots**, of the same patterns as established at this time for lower ranks of Grenadier and Musketeer regiments, and along with this, these regiments are ordered to have **shoulder straps** and **epaulettes** with the numbers of their divisions. In those cases where there are two Jäger regiments in a division, shoulder straps and epaulettes are prescribed to be red for the senior of them, and sky blue for the junior; where there is only one Jäger regiment, these are to be red (806).

14 March 1808—When in formation, lower ranks of Jäger regiments are ordered to have muskets with **fixed bayonets** (807).

7 May 1808— All Jäger regiments are ordered to have white **collars**, piped red, on their present dark-green coats. **Cuffs** are red (Illus. 1388); **pants** are dark green with red piping in the side seam (808).

25 June 1808—All lower ranks of Jäger regiments are ordered to have muskets with **three-edged bayonets**, while rifles and sword-bayonets are not to be used (809).

2 November 1808—The summer and winter **pants** established on 23 December 1807 are to be kept only for combatant lower ranks, while noncombatants are ordered to have pants as well as boots of the pattern introduced in 1802 (810).

11 February 1809—Noncombatant lower ranks who do not hold noncommissioned-officer rank are given new-pattern *caps* [*shapki*] in place of their previous shakos [*kivera*] and forage caps with tassels, the same as those introduced at this time in Grenadier and Musketeer regiments, with the only difference being that their cap band is not red, but dark green with red piping along the top edge (811).

13 February 1809—In all Jäger regiments **collars** (instead of white) and **cuffs** (instead of red) are ordered to be dark green, the same color as the coat, with red piping, which is also kept on the cuff flaps (Illus. 1389) (812).

4, 8, and 20 August 1809—The directive that noncommissioned officers have **galloon** on the top edge of the collar instead of the bottom, and the changes in the fitting of **musket slings** and in the pattern and wear of **knapsacks**, described above for Grenadier regiments, were all extended with equal force to Jäger regiments, with the only difference being that for the last the knapsack straps were black (Illus. 1389) (813).

24 May 1809—Field and company grade officers of Jäger regiments are given *gorgets* [*znaki*] of the same pattern as used at this time by field and company-grade officers of Grenadier and Musketeer regiments (814).

8 and 11 June 1809—The changes in the pattern of **hats** for generals and the addition of cords to lower ranks' **shakos**, as described above for Grenadier regiments, are applied with equal force to Jäger regiments (Illus. 1389) (815).

8 July 1809—All Jäger regiments with red **shoulder straps** are to have them in yellow (816).

23 November 1809—Combatant lower ranks of Jäger regiments are given **pompons** [*repeiki*] for their shakos, identical to those established at this time for Grenadier and Musketeer regiments, while the previous upper tufts [*kistochki*] in the form of small plumes [*sultanchiki*] are abolished (817).

6 December 1809—Jäger field and company-grade officers are ordered to have, when in formation, *shakos* [*kivera*] instead of hats, of the same pattern as confirmed at this time for field and company-grade officers of Grenadier regiments, but without plumes and grenades, with a brass chain on the chinstrap, fixed tightly to one side of the shako and and fastened on the other with a hook to a small gilt star (Illus. 1390).

In this same year Jäger generals and officers received permission to wear *frock coats* [*sertuki*] of the same style as established for Grenadier and Musketeer regiments, dark green in color, with the same colored lining and red piping on the collar and cuffs; **powdered hair** was completely abolished (Illus. 1390) (818).

31 December 1809—All Jäger regiments are ordered to have brass numerals on their cartridge pouches corresponding to the number of the regiment (819).

9 January 1810—The **shakos** in all Jäger regiments are to have a brass grenade with one flame, instead of the ribbon, and **shoulder straps** —with the divisional number—are as follows:

1st Jäger Regiment- yellow, with a N°2; *2nd* - yellow, with N°21; *3rd* - yellow, with N°6; *4th* - yellow with N°4; *5th* - yellow, with N°7; *6th* - yellow, with N°12; *7th* - yellow, with N°8; *8th* - yellow, with N°10; *9th* - sky blue, with N°20; *10th* - yellow, with N°9; *11th* - yellow, with N°11; *12th* - yellow, with N°13; *13th* - sky blue, with N°15; *14th* - yellow, with N°15; *15th* - yellow, with N°20; *16th* - yellow, with N°19; *17th* -sky blue, with N°19; *18th* - yellow, with N°24; *19th* - yellow, with N°25; *20th* - yellow, with N°3; *21st* - sky blue, with N°3; *22nd* - sky blue, with N°13; *23rd* - yellow, with N°5; *24th* - sky blue, with N°5; *25th* - yellow, with N°14; *26th* - sky blue, with N°14; *27th* - yellow, with N°16; *28th* - yellow, with N°18; *29th* - yellow, with N°22; *30th* - yellow, with N°17; *31st* - sky blue, with N°17; *32nd* - sky blue, with N°18 (820).

25 November 1810—Grenadiers and Marksmen of Jäger regiments are given **swords** [*tesaki*] patterned after the swords in the rest of the Army infantry (821).

17 January 1811—Noncommissioned officers and musicians of Jäger regiments are ordered to have white**cords** on their shakos instead of multicolored ones, while the cords' tassels are to have a mix of black and orange (822).

4 February 1811—Grenadiers and Marksmen are ordered to have hair **plumes** on their shakos, of the same pattern as those confirmed at this time for Grenadier regiments: for privates —all black; for noncommissioned officers—black with a white top with an orange stripe down its middle; for drummers and fifers —all red; for musicians—red with the same top as for noncommissioned officers (823).

The following directives, described above, for Grenadier and Musketeer regiments were also applied to Jäger regiments: **22 February 1811** —about pompon colors in all companies and swordknot colors in Grenadier companies, and also about Marksmen not wearing plumes; **8 April 1811** — about Grenadiers and Marksmen having three-flamed grenades on their shakos; **5 April 1811** —about noncombatant noncommissioned officers being authorized swordknots for their swords; **23 September 1811** —concerning the change in forage caps for combatant ranks; and **9 October** and **3 November 1811** —about canes and gloves being taken away from noncommissioned officers. These applied the Jäger regiments, the only difference being that the forage caps had dark-green bands, as in Marine regiments (824).

7 November 1811—In the Jäger regiments of the newly established **27th Division** shoulder straps are to be: in the *49th* - yellow, in the *50th* - dark blue (825).

The folowing directives, described above for Grenadier regiments, were also applicable to Jäger regiments: **11 December 1811** —about the new uniform for noncombatant lower ranks; **1 January 1812** - about the new pattern shakos, the changes in the styles of collars, leggings (Illus. 1391), and officers' boots, and officers having white appointments and brass, forged epaulettes; and **10 February 1812** —about noncombatant lower ranks wearing shoulder straps (826).

12 April 1812—The 20th, 4th, 23rd, 3rd, 11th, 7th, 10th, 8th, 1st, 6th, 12th, 25th, 13th, 27th, 30th, 28th, 16th, 9th, 2nd, 29th, 18th, 19th, 31st, 5th, and 49th Jäger regiments, being the senior in their brigades, are assigned yellow **shoulder straps**, while all the rest are to have sky-blue ones (827).

13 April 1813—The 1st, 5th, 14th, and 20th Jäger regiments are awarded **badges** for their shakos with the inscription "For excellence" (*"Za otlichie"*), identical to those awarded to Grenadier and Musketeer regiments. The pattern for these was used for all Jäger regiments which received this award later during the reign of Emperor Alexander I (828).

22 August 1814—The senior Jäger regiments in brigades are to have sky-blue **shoulder straps** (instead of yellow), while the junior regiments (instead of blue) are to have dark-green ones with red piping (829).

The following directives, described above for Grenadier and Infantry regiments, were also applied to Jäger regiments: **1814 and 1815** —about changes in the patterns for officers' riding trousers and the cockade on officers' hats, and about the uniform for drum majors, musicians, fifers, and drummers; **24 January 1816** —about rapiers and swords having black scabbards; **7 May 1816** —about drum majors wearing uniforms with silver galloon; **13 May 1816** — concerning the introduction of covers for shakos, plumes, coats, etc.; **8 August 1817** —about the size of the forage cap; and **26 September 1817** —about instructions for the construction and wear of shakos and other accouterments. These applied to Jäger regiments but with the following differences from the previously described Army infantry:

1.) Stripes on the riding trousers of Jäger officers were to be black, while the piping on the side seams was to be red (Illus. 1392).

2.) On the covers for shakos and plumes and on the bands of forage caps for Carabinier companies (formerly Grenadiers) of Jäger regiments, the writing,—instead of Cyrillic 1 G.R., 2 G.R., 3 G.R.—was to be: Cyrillic 1 K.R., 2 K.R., 3 K.R., while yellow brass numerals were to be on the covers of pouches, as before, designating the regimental number.

3.) Shakos and drummers' crossbelts in Carabinier companies were to be as in Grenadier companies of Musketeer regiments, while in Jäger companies they were to be as in the Musketeer companies of these regiments (Illus. 1393 and 1394).

4.) Swordbelts, crossbelts, and in general all accouterment straps in Jäger regiments were to be of black, polished leather; these were also to be stitched along the sides, as in Grenadier and Musketeer regiments (830).

3 February 1816—Officers' coats in Jäger regiments are not to have **pocket flaps** across the tails (831).

8 December 1817—Jäger regiments are given **leggings with spats**.

In this same year, those Jäger regiments which were in the **Separate Lithuania Corps** were ordered to have: instead of yellow appointments—white, instead of red piping —yellow, instead of dark-green cuff flaps—yellow, and, in addition, they were given dark-green cloth plastrons for their coats, with yellow piping (Illus. 1395 and 1396). Officers' shabracks and holsters were also to have yellow piping instead of red, and with silver galloon instead of gold (Illus. 1397) (832).

23 August 1818—The instructions issued on this date concerning the size and form of musketeer **shoulder straps** are also applicable to Jäger regiments, with the only difference being that these last had them, as before, in only two colors: blue [*svetlosinii*] and dark green; in both cases with yellow divisional numbers (833).

4 April 1819—The spats that were part of the leggings are eliminated (834).

10 April 1819—The *hornists* [*gornisty*] or *signalers* [*signalisty*] introduced into the personnel tables for Jäger regiments are prescribed the same uniform as drummers, while the **signal horns** [*signalnye rozhki*] are of the same pattern as for grenadiers and musketeers except with black straps instead of white, and painted green inside instead of red (835). The following directives, described above for Grenadier and Musketeer regiments, were also extended to Jäger regiments: **20 September 1820** —about the change in officers' gorgets; **26 September 1823** —about all musicians having noncommissioned-officers' distinctions, and in this same year —about pompons being introduced for shakos; **16 January 1824** —about the changes in shako cords, knapsack straps, and musket shoulder straps; and **29 March 1825** —about the tape sewn onto the left sleeve for faultless service (836).

V. GRENADIER JÄGER, OR CARABINIER, REGIMENTS.

3 April 1814— With the renaming of the *1st, 3rd, 8th, 14th, 26th,* and *29th Jäger regiments* as **Grenadier Jägers** [*Grenaderskie Yegerskie*], there was no change in their uniform.

22 August 1814— These regiments are ordered to have yellow **shoulder straps** with their previous divisional numbers in red cloth. Furthermore, all the directives described above for Jäger regiments were also applicable to them: **1814** and **1815** — about the changes in the pattern for officers' riding trousers and the cockade on officers' hats, and about uniforms for drum majors, fifers, and drummers, as well as about the pattern for the shako badges for distinction; **24 January 1816** — about rapiers and swords having black scabbards; and **3 February 1816** — about officers' coats not having pocket flaps (837). During this time, on **30 August 1815** and **12 February 1816**, the six regiments mentioned above, and also the 17th Jägers, were, as already stated, named: *1st, 2nd, 3rd, 4th, 5th, 6th,* and *7th Carabiniers* (838).

16 April 1818— Carabinier regiments are given plates for their shakos, of the same pattern as those confirmed at this time for Grenadier regiments (838).

7 May, 8 August, and 26 September 1817— The directive for drum majors to have silver galloon on their coats; the defining of forage-cap dimensions, and the instructions for constructing and wearing shakos and other accouterments—were all extended to Carabinier regiments, with the following differences as opposed to Jägers:

    1.) Shakos were to be of the same pattern as for Grenadiers, with the plates established on 16 April 1817 and with curved chin scales; with plumes in Carabinier platoons and without them in the rest. On the cover of the cartridge pouch, in place of the previous grenade, plates were issued, of yellow brass and similar to the shako badge for distinction, with a raised regimental number and the letter K. (Illus. 1398).

    2.) Drummers' crossbelts in all companies were ordered to have three grenades, as in Grenadier regiments (839).

8 December 1817— Carabinier regiments are to have **spats** on their **leggings** (840).

23 March 1818— **Shoulder straps** in Carabinier regiments are to be yellow, as before, and with the number not of the division but of the regiment. Their pattern is to be the same as the shoulder straps established at this time for Grenadier regiments, the uniform for musicians also being exactly the same as in these regiments (Illus. 1399) (841). For the **Carabinier Regiment of the Separate Lithuania Corps**, newly formed in this same year, all uniforms, accouterments, and armaments were authorized to be of the patterns for the Jägers of this corps, with those differences that existed between Carabinier and Jäger regiments in the rest of the Army infantry, plus the additional distinction that Marksmen and Jägers of this regiment had shakos with the pompons described above for the uniforms of Infantry and Jäger regiments of the Lithuanian Corps (Illus. 1400). Shoulder straps on the coats of this regiment had the Cyrillic letter L., but with its being renamed the *Nesvizh Carabiniers* in 1824, these had the Cyrillic letter N., which was also applied to the plates on the cartridge pouches with the addition of the letter K. (842).

All the directives after this time, already described above for Jäger regiments, were also applied in full to Carabinier regiments: **4 April 1819** — about spats being eliminated on leggings; **10 April 1819** — about the uniform for signalers and the pattern for signal horns; **20 September 1823** — about musicians having noncommissioned officers' distinctions, and in this same year—about the pompons introduced for the shako; **16 January 1824** —about the changes in shako cords, knapsack straps, and musket shoulder straps; and **29 March 1825** — about the tape sewn onto the left sleeve in recognition of faultless service (843).

Notes to the Illustrations, by Mark Conrad

Frontispiece: Emperor Alexander I. This portrait depicts the Tsar at the end of his reign wearing an undress uniform of a general of the Cavalier Guard Regiment. The coat is dark green with red piping and silver buttons and epaulettes, the shoulder boards of these last being backed with red.

1274. The plates in Volume 10 continue with the numbering of the previous volumes, each volume averaging something over a hundred illustrations. Viskovatov supervised the production of a team of artists and engravers. This particular plate is credited to Gubarev, Berestov, and Giller. Other persons credited with their work in Volume 10 include Zakharov, Pashennyi, Razumikhin, Anderson, Petrovskii, Fernlyund, Ratye, and Schmidt.

1276. The grenadier under arms has his hair powdered, while his comrade's is unpowdered.

1277. Both grenadiers have powdered hair.

1279. Even the young fifer has white powdered hair. The straps of the fife case are white. Viskovatov says that the pompon for this regiment was white, but Zvegintsov says that it had a red center. In this plate, the fifer's pompon has a colored center in his pompon but the drummer's is all white.

1288. As a bit of trivia, the Russian word *lekar* has the same root as the old English word for a doctor— "leech".

1293-4. I have no explanation why this and other plates have more than one number.

1297-8. Zvegintsov writes, "4 August 1804. <u>Hat.</u> For officers the button loop was to be of narrow galloon, either gold or silver according to the uniform's appointments (instead of with a star as previously), and instead of a ribbon there was prescribed a round cockade of black tape with orange checks. The plume was higher than before, but the color was unchanged."

1328. The cuffs on the drum major's coat appears to be red with a flap. This flap has tassels on one side and a strip of lace under three buttons on the other. That strip of lace appears to be longer than the flap and joins a horizontal strip of lace on the sleeve. This second strip of lace passes the top of the flap lace to make a right angle down the rear seam of the sleeve. The collar of the coat has NCO lace on the front and top, and musician's lace on the bottom.

1329. The words *"Za veru i vernost"* translate as "For faith and fidelity".

1383. If the jäger leaning on the fence appears bemused, perhaps it is because he has two right hands!

SOME NEW INFORMATION REGARDING GRENADIER UNIFORMS, 1802-1806.

According to research by Petr Kosmolinskii and published in the Russian magazine *Tseikhgauz*, No. 3 (1/1994), the true colors for grenadier uniforms from 1802 to 1806 were those of a table of 27 May 1802, signed by Lieutenant General Prince Dolgorukov. This is confirmed by surviving examples of grenadier caps. Viskovatov's (and hence Zvegintsov's) information was apparently from a *proposed* scheme different from Dolgorukov's which was the one actually adopted. In fact, the order of 6 June 1802 that Viskovatov cites as his source was examined by Kosmolinskii and found to be the scheme of Dolgorukov. Viskovatov had made an error and while citing the correct order, provided the wrong scheme.

The following is from Kosmolinskii's research and lists the inspectorates and each one's regiments in order. The inspectorate color was for collars, cuffs (cuff flaps always dark green), and the upper back of the grenadier cap. In each inspectorate the regiments had the distinguishing colors (in order) of red, white, yellow, light raspberry, turquoise, rose, light green, grey, lilac, and dark blue. Red was for the first regiment of an inspectorate, white for the second, and so on up to however many colors were needed based on the number of regiments in the inspectorate. These regimental distinguishing colors were for the shoulder strap, lower band around the grenadier cap, and the middle of the pompon on the cap (except here raspberry was replaced by light green). Exceptions are noted.

INSPECTORATE — Inspectorate color - Regiments (in order)

FINLAND — yellow - Velikie-Luki [*Velikolutskii*], Ryazan, Neva.

ST. PETERSBURG — red - Life-Grenadiers, Pavlovsk Grenadiers, Kexholm, Belozersk (black band), Yelets, Tenginsk (dark-blue band), Lithuania, Petrovsk (dark-green; formed 16.05.1803).

LIVONIA [*LIVLAND, LIFLYANDSKII*] — turquoise - St.-Petersburg Grenadiers, Taurica Grenadiers, Chernigov, Tobolsk, Sevsk, Dnieper, Reval, Sofiya, Kopore (spelled *Kaporskii* by Kosmolinskii; formed 16.05.1803 with the normal ninth-place color of lilac, placed as the *tenth* regiment of the inspectorate on 21.06.05 with violet strap, band, and pompon middle, the Kopore's place being taken by the Kaluga Regiment which was formed 29.08.05 and which had the usual ninth-place lilac).

LITHUANIA [*LITOVSKII*] — light green - Yekaterinoslav Grenadiers, Pskov, Rostov, Murom, Archangel, Nizovsk, Tula, Volhynia (formed 16.05.1803, place taken by the Mogilev which was formed 29.08.05), Kostroma (formed 29.08.1805), Volhynia (since 21.06.1805 with dark-green strap, band, and pompon middle).

BREST — straw - Azov, Viborg, Old-Ingermanland, Apsheron, Ryazhsk, Podolia, Vilna, Penza.

UKRAINE — rose - Kiev Grenadiers (black band), Little-Russia Grenadiers, Smolensk, Bryansk (rose band), Galich (formed 16.05.1803, place taken by the Estonia [Estland] which was formed 29.08.05), Galich (since 21.06.1805 with sky-blue strap, band, and pompon middle).

DNIESTER — lilac (dark green since 15.11.1804) - Siberia Grenadiers, Kherson Grenadiers, Nizhnii-Novgorod, Vladimir (black band), Yaroslavl, Ladoga, Aleksopol, Kozlov, New Ingermanland, Crimea (formed 16.05.1803).

Since 21.06.1805 this inspectorate was reorganized as: Nizhnii-Novgorod, Vladimir, Yaroslavl, Aleksopol, Kozlov, New Ingermanland, Crimea, Odessa.

CRIMEA — blanched (i.e. dull tan or flesh color) - Troitsk, Vitebsk, Belev (black band), Sevastopol (light-green band). Since 21.06.1805 this inspectorate was reorganized as: Siberia Grenadiers, Kherson Grenadiers, Troitsk, Vitebsk, Ladoga, Belev.

CAUCASUS — dark blue - Caucasus Grenadiers, Kazan, Suzdal, Tiflis, Kabarda, Saratov (the Kura Regiment was formed on 29.12.1802 and in the Moscow Inspectorate took the place of the Saratov, which at the same time was transferred to the Caucasus Inspectorate; the Saratov's place in this inspectorate was taken by the Sevastopol on 21.06.1805), Vologda (formed 16.05.1803), Saratov (in this position since 21.06.1805).

SMOLENSK — white - Moscow Grenadiers, Phanagoria Grenadiers, Perm, Voronezh, Uglich, Kursk, Polotsk.

KIEV — light raspberry - Moscow (black band), Novgorod, Vyatka, Narva, Butyrsk, Kolyvan (dark-blue band), Poltava.

MOSCOW — orange - Astrakhan Grenadiers (black band), Schlüsselburg, Nasheburg, Tambov (orange band), Orel, Staryi-Oskol (dark-green band), Navaginsk, Ukraine, Saratov (replaced by the newly formed Kura Regiment on 29.12.1802), Olonets.

ORENBURG — camel (i.e. light brown) - Rylsk, Ufa, Yekaterinburg.

SIBERIA — grey - Shirvan, Tomsk, Selenginsk.

The outsides of pompons were white for the 1st Battalion of the Life-Grenadiers and all Musketeer regiments, yellow for the 2nd Battalion, and red for the 3rd. In the rest of the Grenadier regiments the outside of the pompons was always white.

Kosmolinskii promised to publish a future article giving the correct colors for jäger and garrison regiments.

NOTES

(750) PSZ, vol. XL, pg. 188, No30,309.
(751) The same sources as shown above for Grenadier regiments, and also the table of uniforms, accouterments, and weapons confirmed by Highest Authority on 30 April 1802.
(752) PSZ, vol. XLIV, part II.
(753) PSZ, vol. XLIV, part II, pg. 30, No20,485.
(754) See above, the description of colors in the article for 6 June 1802.
(755) See above, note 672.
(756) See above, note 673.
(757) See above, note 674.
(758) Information from the Government Military College to the Military Commission, 3 August 1804.
(759) Information from the Government Military College to the Military Commission, 31 December. See above, note 672.
(760) See above, note 673.
(761) PSZ, vol. XLIV, part II, pg. 67, No21,589.
(762) See above, note 677.
(763) See above, note 678.
(764) See above, note 680.
(765) PSZ, vol. XLIV, pg. 70, No21,987.
(766) See above, notes 678 and 679.
(767) PSZ, vol. XLIV, pg. 70, No22,373.
(768) See all these articles above for Grenadier regiments.
(769) PSZ, vol. XLIV, pg. 68, No24,113.
(770) See these articles for Grenadier regiments.
(771) PSZ, vol. XLIV, part II, pg. 71, No24,861.
(772) See these articles for Grenadier regiments.
(773) Ukase of the Military College, for 1812.
(774) Highest Order.
(775) See these articles for Grenadier regiments.
(776) See these articles for Grenadier regiments, and PSZ, vol. XLIV, part II, pg. 101, No27,067.
(777) and (778) See these articles for Grenadier regiments, and drawings as well as uniforms themselves of the former Separate Lithuania Corps, still preserved.
(779) PSZ.
(780) See these articles for Grenadier regiments.
(781) A personnel table and chart for a Marine regiment, confirmed by Highest Authority on 29 April 1803, with later changes after this, and

evidence from contemporaries.

(782) See for Musketeer regiments.

(783) PSZ, vol. XLIV, part I, section II, pp. 42, 86, and 96, No21,794, and information extracted from transactions of the Commissariat Department of the Ministry of War.

(784) PSZ, vol. XXVI, pg. 609, No19,826.

(785) PSZ, vol. XLIV, part II, pg. section IV, pg. 71, No19,874.

(786) See the description for Grenadier regiments.

(787) Table of uniforms, accouterments, and weapons for Army Jäger regiments, confirmed by Highest Authority, and PSZ, vol. XLIV, part II, pg. 30, No20,186; pg. 71, No20,109; and pg. 64, No20,287.

(788) PSZ, vol. XLIV, part II, pg. 64, No20,287.

(789) Information from the Government Military College, 16 September 1802, and an actual model headdress held by the Commissariat Department of the Ministry of War.

(790) Information from the Government Military College to the Military Commission, from 22 June 1803.

(791) PSZ, vol. XLIV, pg. 71, No21,117, and contemporary drawings and evidence.

(792) PSZ, vol. XXVIII, pg. 264, No21,258.

(793) Decision by the Government Military College, from 4 August 1804, and evidence from contemporaries.

(794) PSZ, vol. XLIII, part II, pg. 38, No21,928.

(795) PSZ, vol. XLIV, pg. 67, No21,969.

(796) PSZ, vol. XLIV, pg. 71, No22,009.

(797) PSZ, vol. XLIV, pg. 71, No22,185.

(798) PSZ, vol. XLIV, pg. 31, No21,197.

(799) PSZ, vol. XXIX, pg. 789, No22,321, and a model cartridge pouch at the Commissariat Department of the Ministry of War.

(800) PSZ, vol. XXIX, pg. 201, No22,382.

(801) PSZ, vol. XLIV, part II, pg. 71, No22,185.

(802) PSZ, vol. XLIV, pg. 14, No22,625.

(803) PSZ, vol. XLIV, pg. 14, No22,633.

(804) PSZ, vol. XLIV, pg. 54, No22,677.

(805) PSZ, vol. XLIV, part II, pg. 13, No22,720, and evidence from contemporaries.

(806) PSZ, vol. XLIV, pg. 67, No22,727.

(807) PSZ, vol. XXX, pg. 128, No22,895.

(808) PSZ, vol. XLIV, pg. 71, No23,005.

(809) PSZ, vol. XLIV, pg. 67, No23,335.

(810) From transactions in the Archive of the Commissariat Department of the Ministry of War.

(811) PSZ, vol. XXX, pg. 781, No23,478.

(812) PSZ, vol. XLIV, pg. 72, No23,481, and a model jäger coat preserved at the Commissariat Department of the Ministry of War.

(813) See this article for Grenadier regiments.

(814) PSZ, vol. XXX, pg. 965, No23,654.

(815) See above in the articles for Grenadier regiments.

(816) PSZ, vol. XLIV, pg. 72, No23,741.

(817) PSZ, vol. XLIV, pg. 68, No24,000.

(818) PSZ, vol. XXX, pg 1362, No24,019, and evidence from contemporaries.

(819) PSZ, vol. XLIV, pg. 72, No24,058.

(820) PSZ, vol. XLIV, pg. 72/68, NoNo24,077/24,113.

(821) PSZ, vol. XXXI, pg. 461, No24,438.

(822) PSZ, vol. XXXI, pg. 517, No24,488.

(823) PSZ, vol. XLIV, pg. 69, No24,509.

(824) See these articles for Grenadier, Musketeer, and Marine regiments.

(825) PSZ, vol. XLIV, pg. 72, No24,861.

(826) See these articles for Grenadier regiments.

(827) Book of Ukases of the Military College, for 1812, pg. 1331.

(828) and (829) Highest Orders.

(830) See these articles for Grenadier regiments, and PSZ, vol. XLIV, part II, pg. 104, No27,067.

(831) PSZ, vol. XLIV, part II, Instructions in regard to uniforms, pg. 103, No26,655.

(832) From transactions in the Archive of the Commissariat Department of the Ministry of War and contemporary drawings.

(833) PSZ, vol. XLIV, part II, pg. 121, No27,504.

(834) and (835) From transactions in the Archive of the Commissariat Department of the Ministry of War.

(836) and (837) See these articles for Grenadier and Musketeer regiments.

(838) PSZ, vol. XLIV, pg. 138, No26,801.

(839) See these articles for Grenadier and Jäger regiments, and PSZ, vol. XLIV, part II, pg. 104, No27,067.

(840) From transactions in the Archive of the Commissariat Department of the Ministry of War.

(841) PSZ, vol. XLIV, part II, pg. 121, No27,504.

(842) From transactions in the Archive of the Commissariat Department of the Ministry of War, and PSZ, vol. XLIV, part II, pg. 103, No27,298.

(843) See these articles for Jäger regiments.

РИСУНКИ ОДЕЖДЫ и ВООРУЖЕНІЯ РОССІЙСКИХЪ ВОЙСКЪ 1801-1825.

PLATES LIST OF ILLUSTRATIONS

1344. Musketeer. Velikie-Luki Musketeer Regiment of the Finland Inspectorate. 1802 and 1803.

1345. Musketeer. Yelets Musketeer Regiment of the St.-Petersburg Inspectorate. 1802-1803.

1346. Musketeer. Sevsk Musketeer Regiment of the Livonia Inspectorate. 1802 and 1803.

1347. Musketeer. Tula Musketeer Regiment of the Lithuania Inspectorate. 1802 and 1803.

1348. Musketeer Noncommissioned Officer. Old-Ingermanland Musketeer Regiment of the Brest Inspectorate. 1802 and 1803.

1349. Musketeer Noncommissioned Officers. Smolensk and Ladoga Musketeer Regiments of the Ukraine and Dniester Inspectorates. 1802 and 1803.

1350. Musketeer Drummer. Belev Musketeer Regiment of the Crimea Inspectorate. 1802 and 1803.

1351. Musketeer Drummers. Polotsk and Suzdal Musketeer Regiments of the Smolensk and Caucasus Inspectorates. 1802 and 1803.

1352. Regimental Drummer. Moscow Musketeer Regiment of the Kiev Inspectorate. 1802-1803.

1353. Musician. Penza Musketeer Regiment of the Moscow Inspectorate. 1802 and 1803.

1354. Company-grade Officer. Rylsk Musketeer Regiment of the Orenburg Inspectorate. 1802-1804.

1355. Noncombatant of Noncommissioned Officer Rank. Shirvan Musketeer Regiment of the Siberia Inspectorate. 1802 and 1803.

1356. Musketeer Noncommissioned Officer. 1803-1805.

1357. Musketeer Shako. 1805-1807.

1358. Musketeer. 1809.

1359. Musketeer. 1812-1817.

1360. Drummer. Musketeer Regiments. 1817-1820.

1361. Noncommissioned Officer and Field-grade Officer. Infantry Regiments of the Separate Lithuania Corps. 1817-1823.

1362. Musketeer. Regiments of the Separate Lithuania Corps. 1825-1828.

1363. Private and Company-grade Officer. Marine Regiments. 1812-1817.

1364. Forage Caps for Marine Regiments, from 1812.

1365. Officers' Shabrack and Holsters for Marine Regiments. 1812.

1366. Grenadier. Marine Regiments. 1817-1826.

1367. Privates. 1st and 2nd Jäger Regiments. 1802-1807.

1368. Privates. 3rd and 4th Jäger Regiments. 1802.

1369. Privates. 5th, 6th, and 7th Jäger Regiments. 1802.

1370. Noncommissioned Officers. 8th and 9th Jäger Regiments. 1802.

1371. Company Drummer. 10th Jäger Regiment. 1802.

1372. Battalion and Regimental Drummers. 11th and 12th Jäger Regiments. 1802.

1373. Waldhornists. 13th and 14th Jäger Regiments. 1802.

1374. Company-grade Officers. 15th and 16th Jäger Regiments. 1802-1804.

1375. Field-grade Officer. 17th Jäger Regiment. 1802-1804.

1376. Generals. 18th and 19th Jäger Regiments. 1802-1804.

1377. Jäger Hat. 1802-1807.

1378. Company-grade Officer. 20th Jäger Regiment. 1803 and 1804.

1379. Company-grade Officer and Private. 21st and 22nd Jäger Regiments. 1805-1807.

1380. Battalion Drummer. 23rd Jäger Regiment. 1806 and 1807.

1381. Noncommissioned Officer and Privates. 24th, 25th, and 26th Jäger Regiments. 1806 and 1807.

1382. Private. 27th Jäger Regiment. 1806 and 1807.

1383. Privates. 28th and 29th Jäger Regiments. 1806 and 1807.

1384. Noncommissioned Officer. 30th Jäger Regiment. 1806-1807.

1385. Company-grade Officers. 31st and 32nd Jäger Regiments. 1806-1808.

1386. Private. Jäger Regiments. 1807.

1387. Officers' Shabrack for Jäger Regiments. From 1807 on.

1388. Private. Jäger Regiments. 1808 and 1809.

1389. Private. Jäger Regiments. 1809-1811.

1390. Company-grade Officers. Jäger Regiments. 1809-1811.

1391. Noncommissioned Officer. Jäger Regiments. 1812-1816.

1392. Company-grade Officer. Jäger Regiments. 1817-1824.

1393. Carabinier. Jäger Regiments. 1817-1826.

1394. Drummer. Jäger Regiments. 1817-1826.

1395. Carabinier. Jäger Regiments of the Separate Lithuania Corps. 1817-1828.

1396. Company-grade Officer. Jäger Regiments of the Separate Lithuania Corps. 1817-1828.

1397. Officers' Shabrack for Jäger Regiments of the Separate Lithuania Corps. 1817-1830.

1398. Cartridge-pouch Plate for Carabinier Regiments, confirmed in 1817.

1399. Musician. Carabinier Regiments. 1817-1820.

1400. Marksman. Nesvizh Carabinier Regiment of the Separate Lithuania Corps. 1818-1828.

1544.

Musketeer. Velikie-Luki Musketeer Regiment of the Finland Inspectorate. 1802 and 1803.

Musketeer. Yelets Musketeer Regiment of the St.-Petersburg Inspectorate. 1802-1803.

Musketeer. Sevsk Musketeer Regiment of the Livonia Inspectorate. 1802 and 1803.

Musketeer. Tula Musketeer Regiment of the Lithuania Inspectorate. 1802 and 1803.

Musketeer Noncommissioned Officer. Old-Ingermanland Musketeer Regiment of the Brest Inspectorate. 1802 and 1803.

Musketeer Noncommissioned Officers. Smolensk and Ladoga Musketeer Regiments of the Ukraine and Dniester Inspectorates. 1802 and 1803.

Musketeer Drummer. Belev Musketeer Regiment of the Crimea Inspectorate. 1802 and 1803.

Musketeer Drummers. Polotsk and Suzdal Musketeer Regiments of the Smolensk and Caucasus Inspectorates. 1802 and 1803.

Regimental Drummer. Moscow Musketeer Regiment of the Kiev Inspectorate. 1802-1803.

Musician. Penza Musketeer Regiment of the Moscow Inspectorate. 1802 and 1803.

Company-grade Officer. Rylsk Musketeer Regiment of the Orenburg Inspectorate. 1802-1804.

1355.

Noncombatant of Noncommissioned Officer Rank. Shirvan Musketeer Regiment of the Siberia Inspectorate. 1802 and 1803.

Musketeer Noncommissioned Officer. 1803-1805.

Musketeer Shako. 1805-1807.

1358.

Musketeer. 1809.

Musketeer. 1812-1817

Drummer. Musketeer Regiments. 1817-1820.

1361.

Noncommissioned Officer and Field-grade Officer. Infantry Regiments of the Separate Lithuania Corps. 1817-1823.

1362.

Musketeer. Regiments of the Separate Lithuania Corps. 1825-1828.

Private and Company-grade Officer. Marine Regiments. 1812-1817.

1364.

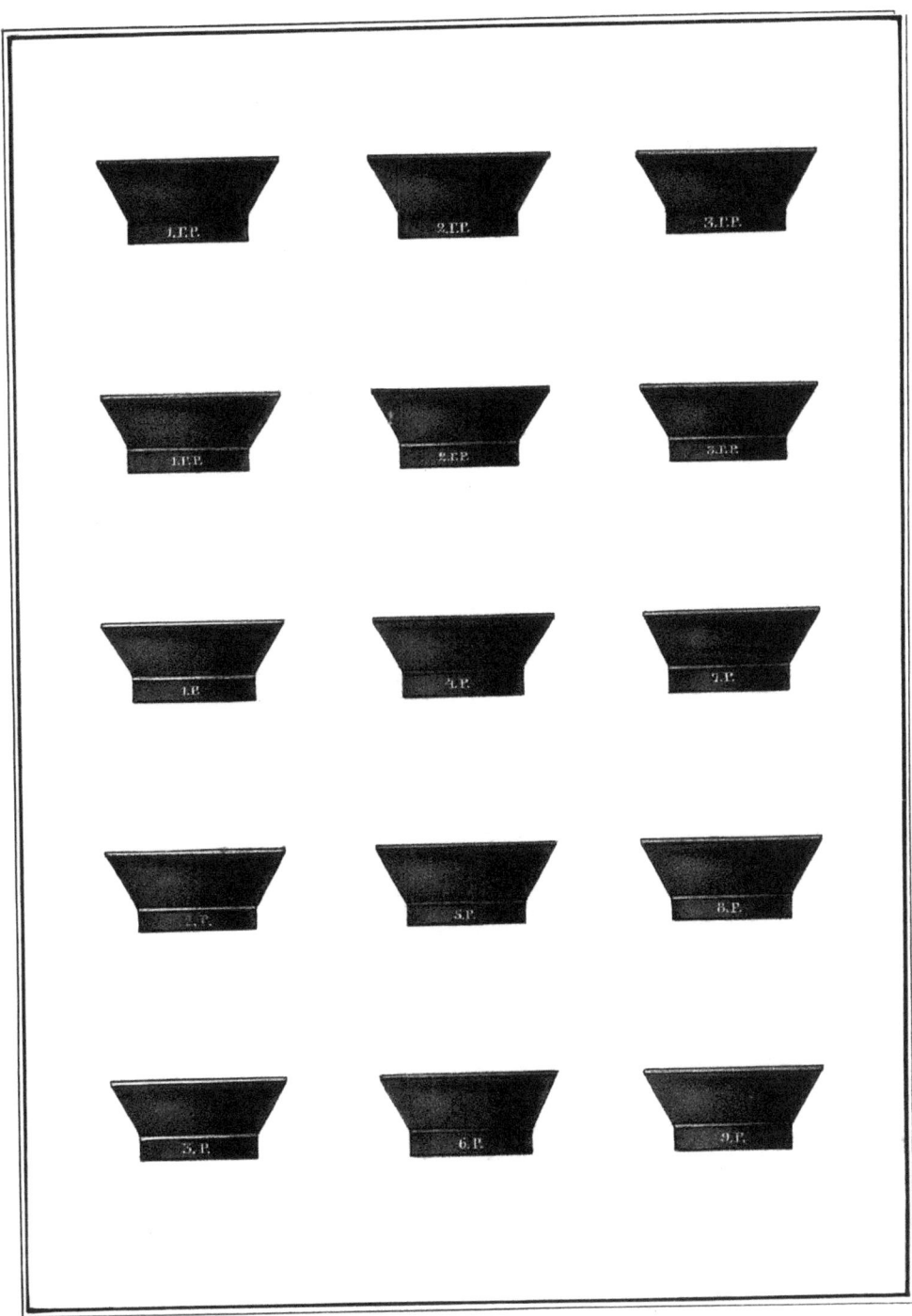

Forage Caps for Marine Regiments, from 1812.

1365.

Officers' Shabrack and Holsters for Marine Regiments. 1812.

1366.

Grenadier. Marine Regiments. 1817-1826.

Privates. 1st and 2nd Jäger Regiments. 1802-1807.

Privates. 3rd and 4th Jäger Regiments. 1802.

1369.

Privates. 5th, 6th, and 7th Jäger Regiments. 1802.

Noncommissioned Officers. 8th and 9th Jäger Regiments. 1802.

Company Drummer. 10th Jäger Regiment. 1802.

Battalion and Regimental Drummers. 11th and 12th Jäger Regiments. 1802.

Waldhornists. 13th and 14th Jäger Regiments. 1802.

Company-grade Officers. 15th and 16th Jäger Regiments. 1802-1804.

Field-grade Officer. 17th Jäger Regiment. 1802-1804.

Generals. 18th and 19th Jäger Regiments. 1802-1804.

1377.

Jäger Hat. 1802-1807.

Company-grade Officer. 20th Jäger Regiment. 1803 and 1804.

Company-grade Officer and Private. 21st and 22nd Jäger Regiments. 1805-1807.

Battalion Drummer. 23rd Jäger Regiment. 1806 and 1807.

Noncommissioned Officer and Privates. 24th, 25th, and 26th Jäger Regiments.
1806 and 1807.

Private. 27th Jäger Regiment. 1806 and 1807.

Privates. 28th and 29th Jäger Regiments. 1806 and 1807.

Noncommissioned Officer. 30th Jäger Regiment. 1806-1807.

1385.

Company-grade Officers. 31st and 32nd Jäger Regiments. 1806-1808.

Private. Jäger Regiments. 1807.

1387.

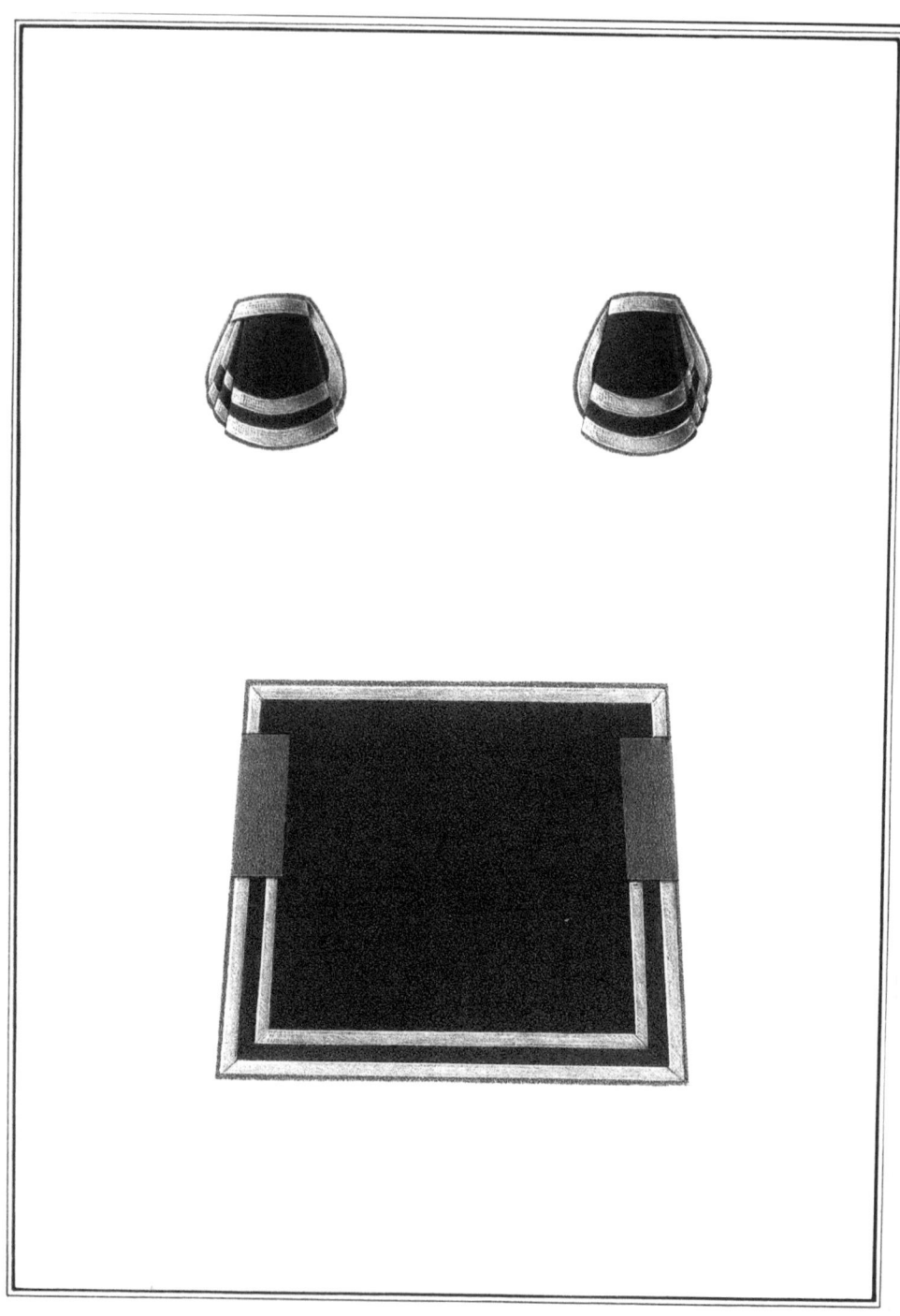

Officers' Shabrack for Jäger Regiments. From 1807 on.

Private. Jäger Regiments. 1808 and 1809.

Private. Jäger Regiments. 1809-1811.

Company-grade Officers. Jäger Regiments. 1809-1811.

Noncommissioned Officer. Jäger Regiments. 1812-1816.

Company-grade Officer. Jäger Regiments. 1817-1824.

Carabinier. Jäger Regiments. 1817-1826.

1394.

Drummer. Jäger Regiments. 1817-1826.

1395.

Carabinier. Jäger Regiments of the Separate Lithuania Corps. 1817-1828.

Company-grade Officer. Jäger Regiments of the Separate Lithuania Corps. 1817-1828.

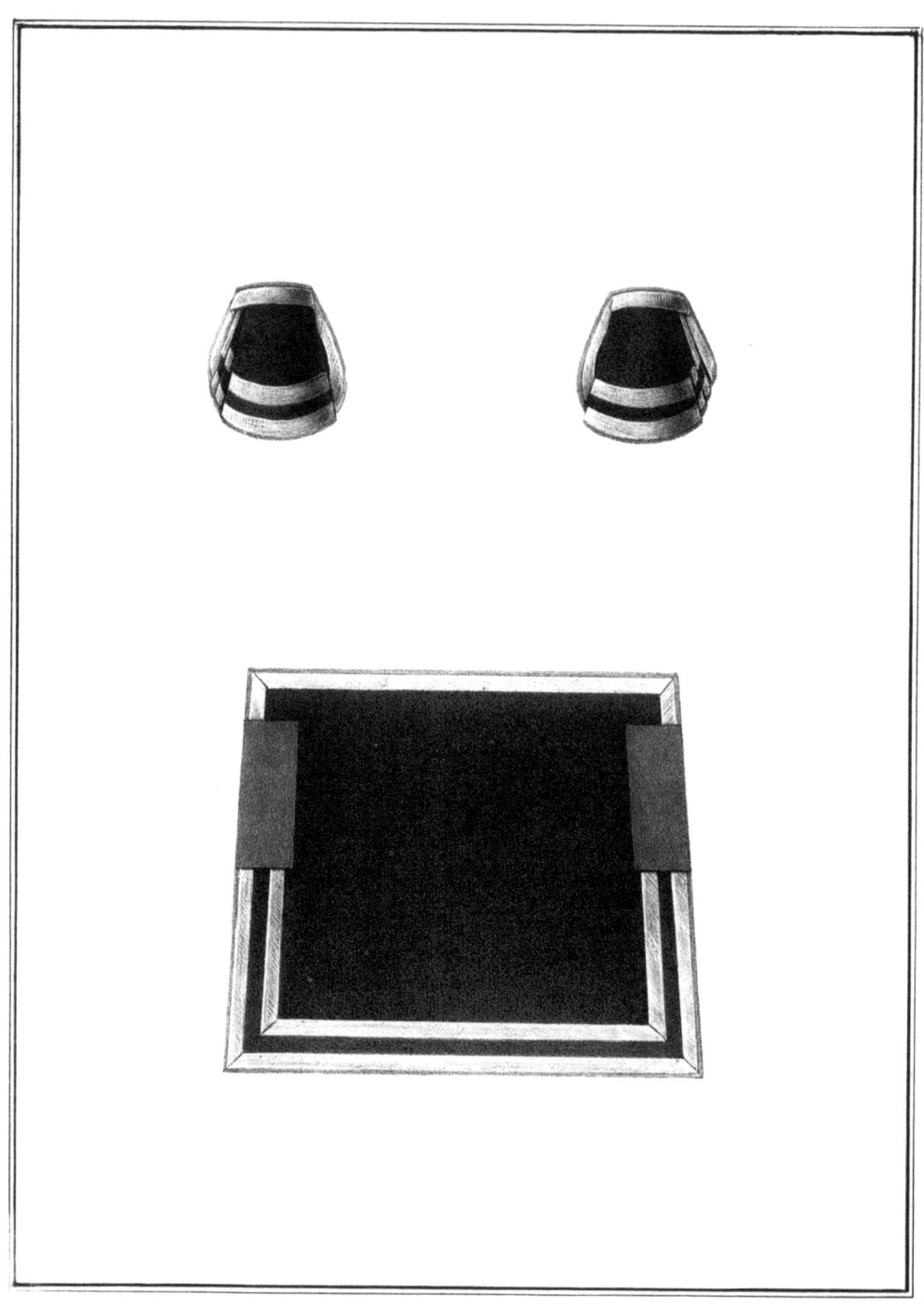

Officers' Shabrack for Jäger Regiments of the Separate Lithuania Corps. 1817-1830.

Cartridge-pouch Plate for Carabinier Regiments, confirmed in 1817.

Musician. Carabinier Regiments. 1817-1820.

Marksman. Nesvizh Carabinier Regiment of the Separate Lithuania Corps. 1818-1828.

WORK PLAN

Our reprint in based on the original 19th century volumes, to be precise the volumes from 7 to 9 are dedicated to the reign of Paul I; this first part is distributed on 7 volumes, having a numbering from 1 to 7. From number 10 to 18 of the original volumes, the second part is dedicated to the Russian troops under Alexander I. These still being worked on and they will be soon ready, distributed on twenty volumes approximately. Our new edition, the first ever published in English, both on paper and digital format, boasts a large number of color plates, many of them unpublished and coloured by our team of expert artists and scholars of uniformology. Each volume is based on 50/70 plates, always accompanied by the original translated text which describes the uniforms, the organization and the armament of the Russian army of the period.

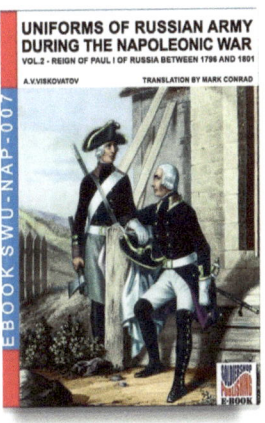

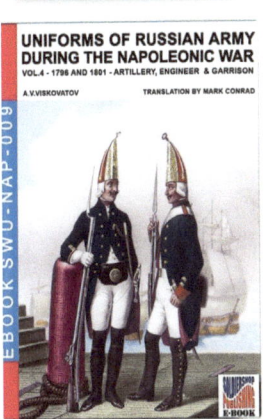